JEREMY GREEN

Jeremy Green's other plays include *Snakes* (Young Vic); an adaptation of *The Fwog Pwince* (BBC Radio); *The Wolfgang Chase* (BBC Radio); *Fairy Tale* and an adaptation of *The Proposal* by Chekhov (Pleasance).

Jeremy Green

LIZZIE SIDDAL

NICK HERN BOOKS
London
www.nickhernbooks.co.uk

A Nick Hern Book

Lizzie Siddal first published in Great Britain in 2014 as a paperback original by Nick Hern Books Limited, The Glasshouse, 49a Goldhawk Road, London W12 8QP

Lizzie Siddal copyright © 2014 Jeremy Green

Jeremy Green has asserted his moral right to be identified as the author of this work

Cover photograph of Emma West as Lizzie Siddal by Rebecca Pitt (www.rebeccapitt.co.uk)

Designed and typeset by Nick Hern Books, London
Printed in Great Britain by Mimeo Ltd, Huntingdon, Cambridgeshire PE29 6XX

A CIP catalogue record for this book is available from the British Library

ISBN   978 1 84842 392 3

MIX
Paper from
responsible sources
FSC® C019549

Lizzie Siddal was first performed at the Arcola Theatre, London, on 20 November 2013. The cast was as follows:

DANTE GABRIEL ROSSETTI	Tom Bateman

JOHN RUSKIN/
   CHARLES HOWELL/
   MR MITCHELL
	Daniel Crossley

WILLIAM HOLMAN HUNT	Simon Darwen
JOHN EVERETT MILLAIS/ MR TEBBS/GREENGROCER	James Northcote
LIZZIE SIDDAL	Emma West
ANNIE MILLER/ GREENGROCER'S MOTHER	Jayne Wisener

Director	Lotte Wakeham
Set and Costume Designer	David Woodhead
Lighting Designer	Howard Hudson
Sound Designer	Andrew Graham
Casting Director	Emma Green
Assistant Director	Georgia Lewis-Smith
Production Manager	Andy Reader
Stage Manager	Anna Sheard
Deputy Stage Manager	Holly Taylor
Assistant Stage Manager	Lily Bootman
Costume Supervisor	Emily Barratt
General Manager	1505 Management
Producers	Copperhead Productions, Peter Huntley Productions
Assistant Producer	Annabel Williamson

For Emma West

*Special thanks to Michael Lindall, to Lotte Wakeham,
and to the late Mr W. J. Stephens*

Characters

CHARLES HOWELL, *thirty*
MR TEBBS, *late twenties*
WILLIAM HOLMAN HUNT, *twenty-five*
LIZZIE SIDDAL, *twenty-two*
DANTE GABRIEL ROSSETTI, *twenty-five*
JOHN EVERETT MILLAIS, *twenty-two*
JOHN RUSKIN, *thirty-three*
ANNIE MILLER, *early twenties*
GREENGROCER, *late twenties*
GREENGROCER'S MOTHER, *mid-forties*
MR MITCHELL, *forty-five*

Note on Text

A forward slash (/) indicates an overlap in dialogue or, when it comes at the end of a line, an abrupt following-on of speech.

ACT ONE

Scene One

*October, 1869. Highgate Cemetery. Night. A mile away, a
church bell strikes the quarter hour.*

CHARLES HOWELL *appears out of the night, carrying
a lantern. Another man with a lantern approaches. It is*
MR TEBBS.

HOWELL. Are you Mr Tebbs?

TEBBS. I am.

HOWELL. Charles Howell. How do you do.

TEBBS. How do you do.

HOWELL. You're very young for a solicitor.

TEBBS. Yes. That's because I'm very good. Are you the man
who's going to put his hands in the coffin?

HOWELL. I am.

TEBBS. Where are the gravediggers?

HOWELL. They went up ahead. The sexton went up with them.

TEBBS. They can't dig before midnight.

HOWELL. They're building a bonfire. For heat and light. Shall
we join them?

They start to go.

TEBBS....What was she like? Do you know?

HOWELL. What was who like?

TEBBS. The woman. The woman we're going to dig up.

HOWELL. Does it matter what she was like?

Scene Two

Lights up on HUNT*'s seedy studio. Morning.*

WILLIAM HOLMAN HUNT *– age twenty-five – paints*
LIZZIE SIDDAL *– age twenty-two. He speaks as he applies oil
paint to a canvas of* A Converted British Family Sheltering a
Christian Missionary.

*She stands motionless, her left arm cradling a wooden bowl,
her right hand poised above the bowl in the act of scooping
water from it. Draped across her shoulders is a green shawl.*

HUNT. Brilliant! The Academy will be compelled to accept this
    because it's *brilliant*! They'll hang it high up, hoping no one
    will notice, but I'm using colour of such intensity, the old
    farts will look up unawares and die of shock. 'Aaaah! It's too
    bright! Where are the shadows? Where's the brown slosh?
    He's not painting with dark-brown slosh! Aargh!' Last to die
    will be Sir Tufton Bufton, wandering in from luncheon. 'By
    Gad! – she's – got – red – hairrrggh!' They hate anything
    different – I *love* anything different. How does it feel to be
    different, Lizzie?

LIZZIE *opens her mouth.*

No, no, don't speak. You know the restriction – models can't
talk in here. I must have no opinion in my head but my own.
An artist's studio cannot be a democracy. Don't be offended.
I am perfecting a new way of living. I call it 'Sincerity'. I
shall paint the truth and speak the truth. I expect to be hated.

ROSSETTI (*off*). Maniac!

HUNT. Not now!

ROSSETTI (*off*). Are you there?

HUNT. I'm working!

ROSSETTI *– age twenty-five – appears in the doorway.
From where he's standing, he can't see* LIZZIE.

ROSSETTI. Are you really working? Or are you gawping at
    pictures of female buttocks?

HUNT....Gabriel, may I present Miss Elizabeth Siddal. Miss Siddal, Mr Rossetti.

ROSSETTI *steps forward and sees her. A beat.*

ROSSETTI (*to* LIZZIE). How do you do... (*To* HUNT.) I thought today was foliage.

HUNT. Friday is foliage. Today is ministering maiden.

ROSSETTI (*to* LIZZIE). Dante Gabriel Rossetti. Or at least a version of him – the embarrassed version. There are other more agreeable versions.

LIZZIE *opens her mouth to reply.*

HUNT. Miss Siddal cannot talk.

ROSSETTI. Really? I'm so sorry.

HUNT. No, I mean, she cannot talk because I am paying her sixpence an hour not to talk, or move. She is working. *I* am working.

ROSSETTI. Yes, but not while I'm here, surely.

HUNT. You don't intend to stay if I'm working?

ROSSETTI. Miss Siddal, what would you think of a man who refuses to converse with his friend merely because of a painting? Can a painting be more important than a person? I think human beings have first claim on our affections, surely.

HUNT. If you've come in search of tin, I don't have any.

ROSSETTI. What makes you think I'm in search of tin?

HUNT. You're always in search of tin.

ROSSETTI. Supposing I were. What's a loan between friends?

HUNT. Debt.

ROSSETTI. You mustn't mind Mr Hunt's temper, Miss Siddal. I am a painter, too. I understand the frustrations painters are prone to.

HUNT. Then why do you stay?

ROSSETTI (*to* LIZZIE). Though I am not only a painter. I am also a poet.

HUNT. Then go and write something.

ROSSETTI. I have. I have been writing. I'm exhausted.

HUNT. What? What have you written in the last three months?

It's a challenge – to a man who hasn't written anything recently. ROSSETTI *hesitates.*

ROSSETTI.
'She fell asleep on Christmas Eve.
At length the long un-granted / shade'

HUNT. That's not a new one, is it?

ROSSETTI. Not strictly new, no.

HUNT. In the last three months.

ROSSETTI. Very well…

'Our Lombard country-girls along the coast
Wear daggers in their garters: for / they know'

HUNT. I heard that last year. It's not new. Nothing recent then?

ROSSETTI.…
'Break, break, break,
On thy cold gray stones, O Sea!
And I would that my tongue could utter
The thoughts that arise in me.

O, well for the fisherman's boy,
That he shouts with his sister at play!
O, well for / the sailor lad.'

LIZZIE (*moving forwards*). But that's not yours!

Both men are surprised.

(*To* HUNT.) …I'm sorry, Mr Hunt. Please take a penny from my wages.

(*To* ROSSETTI.) Tennyson wrote that poem.

ROSSETTI. He did.

LIZZIE. Then why call it yours?

ROSSETTI. I shouldn't have. It was wrong. Perhaps because my own poetry lately is so feeble, I wouldn't dream of airing it on first acquaintance with a lady.

LIZZIE (*disarmed*)....Oh.

HUNT *groans*.

ROSSETTI. But you like Tennyson?

LIZZIE. Yes. Yes, I do. I think him the finest poet we have had since Keats.

ROSSETTI. You like Keats?

LIZZIE. I revere Keats.

ROSSETTI. Keats is fine, isn't he?

LIZZIE. He is beyond / fine.

ROSSETTI. 'A thing of beauty is a joy for ever:'

LIZZIE. 'Its loveliness increases.'

ROSSETTI. 'It will never pass into / nothingness.'

HUNT. Oh, for Christ's sake! (*To* ROSSETTI.) *Now* do you see why I pay people *not* to talk? Suddenly the room is full of opinions! I don't want opinions – hers, or yours! I come here to work! This is *my* studio, *my* painting, mine, mine, mine!

LIZZIE. I'm sorry, Mr Hunt.

ROSSETTI. Never apologise for championing a poet, Miss / Siddal.

HUNT. She was apologising for interrupting a painter!

ROSSETTI. Are you a poet, too, Miss Siddal?

LIZZIE *opens her mouth to reply*.

HUNT. She's a seamstress.

ROSSETTI (*to* LIZZIE). Have you never tried to write poems?

HUNT. No, she sews. And sometimes picks up money modelling, but only when she stands still and keeps quiet.

ROSSETTI (*to* LIZZIE). I haven't seen you before.

HUNT. Gabriel, Gabriel. If you wish to hold a conversation with Miss Siddal, may I suggest later you take an omnibus down the Old Kent Road?

ROSSETTI (*to* LIZZIE). Is that where you live?

HUNT. Why do you keep asking *her* questions? *I'm* talking to you. (*To* LIZZIE.) Don't answer his questions. (*To* ROSSETTI.) What do you want to know? She lives with her parents south of the river Dad's got a shop sells knives and forks thinks he's gentry doesn't know his daughter models when she isn't sewing in a hat shop ribbons mostly on bonnets pleasant girl red hair very useful reads a lot but otherwise unremarkable yours for sixpence an hour do you have sixpence of course you don't I do. 'That is all ye know and all ye need to know' – Keats.

ROSSETTI....I wonder you are not employed at the docks squeezing large cargo into small holds. You cannot compress a life into a minute's breath. It is dismissive. One might even be tempted to call it rude.

LIZZIE. Mr Rossetti. You are kind to leap to my defence where none is needed. Mr Hunt is trying to compress time, not me. It is his money that's at stake – his canvas that needs attention. Any roughness in his manner will be amply compensated by the brilliance of the painting he will bring into the world.

ROSSETTI....My God, but that is beautifully spoken. Where did you learn to speak like that?

HUNT (*warning him*). Gabriel.

ROSSETTI. Is it not nobly said?

HUNT. She reads books.

ROSSETTI. She took your part.

HUNT. I'm paying her.

ROSSETTI. I'm not surprised. I'd pay her, too, to speak so well of me.

HUNT (*exploding*). *What is the reason you are here? What?* I have a work of art that will not wait. It must be done in time. I can't come out to play. What do you want from me?

ROSSETTI (*like a pathetic little boy*). Company.

HUNT *groans*.

HUNT. There are six weeks left. Don't you have your own painting?

ROSSETTI. I have nothing. And even if I had something, the 'Greybeards' would only criticise me, and I hate criticism. I like praise.

HUNT. Then stay home and show your work to your mum. No wonder you live there. 'Look, Mama, here's what I did.' 'Oh it's lovely, Gabriel.' 'And here's what else I did.' 'Oh it's lovely, too, Gabriel.'

ROSSETTI. In point of fact I do have one idea I have long considered.

HUNT. Which one?

ROSSETTI. Beatrice Portinari.

HUNT. Then paint the woman. What's stopping you?

ROSSETTI. I could never find a face to fit. (*To* LIZZIE.) Beatrice Portinari was the love of the great poet, Dante Alighieri. Do you know the story?

LIZZIE. No, / I...

HUNT (*stopping him from telling the story*). No. No.

ROSSETTI. Dante said that from the moment he saw her, he felt his destiny was fixed. When Cupid's arrow strikes, Miss Siddal, the wounded carries the wound for life, there is no remedy. Once we fall in love, we love for ever. Dante loved Beatrice from a distance.

HUNT. Pretty pointless way to love somebody.

ROSSETTI. What could be more moving than love unrequited? A life full of yearning! One day in the street, because of a stupid misunderstanding, Beatrice refused Dante her greeting as she passed by. It broke his heart.

HUNT. The end.

ROSSETTI. She had red hair.

A beat.

HUNT. I don't know if you've noticed, Gabriel, but Miss Siddal is not available *at the moment*.

ROSSETTI. I will have money next week to pay a model's wages. My aunt has promised to send me a guinea. (*To* LIZZIE.) I have a studio in Highgate.

HUNT. What a pity. Miss Siddal tells me on Monday she goes back to work at the hat shop. The bonnet-making season has returned, which is excellent news for ladies with bad hair – and good news for women who sew who need money to eat. You've never had a sweetheart, Gabriel. You think they live on sighs and sonnets. They don't, she doesn't, she works. And so do I, so please, please, please, for the love of God, *leave me to work*!

ROSSETTI.…Of course. You only had to say. Miss Siddal. I do hope we meet again. (*Leaving*.) Maniac.

LIZZIE. Mr Rossetti. There has been an unexpected change in my circumstances. I will be available next week, if that is of any interest.

ROSSETTI. Really?

LIZZIE. Yes.

ROSSETTI. Well. That's remarkable news, isn't it.

Scene Three

ROSSETTI*'s studio; a tiny cottage at the back of a garden in Highgate. A summer morning.*

ROSSETTI *is adjusting the position of a chair, an easel, his hair, his clothes. Truth be told, he's a virgin and not quite as confident as he appeared in the previous scene. Suddenly a button falls from his trousers.*

ROSSETTI. Oh, God.

He retrieves the button and bends over trying to see which part of his trousers the button issued from. LIZZIE appears in the doorway.

LIZZIE. Good morning, sir.

ROSSETTI (*startled*). Miss Siddal. Sorry, a... button fell off.

LIZZIE. Take it to a seamstress.

ROSSETTI. Yes... I don't suppose / you.

LIZZIE. No.

ROSSETTI. No.

LIZZIE. You would have to remove your trousers.

ROSSETTI. Good God. Out of the question.

LIZZIE. Besides, I am not a seamstress this week.

ROSSETTI. Of course you're not. You're a picture. Won't you come in? And please call me Gabriel.

LIZZIE. I'd like that, thank you. I'm Lizzie.

ROSSETTI. Lizzie, the model who reads Keats – which is astonishing.

LIZZIE. Why?

ROSSETTI. Well, that you can read at all is fairly astonishing. Most models can't.

LIZZIE. My father insisted. All his daughters had to learn to read.

ROSSETTI. How many daughters does he have?

LIZZIE. Five.

ROSSETTI. Five? Good grief.

LIZZIE. Why good grief?

ROSSETTI. I have two sisters and they're a handful. And daughters are always more trouble, aren't they.

LIZZIE. Are they?

ROSSETTI. Well, no, not trouble, but expense. There's the dowry for a start. I mean, five!

LIZZIE. That was my father's plan. Instead of a dowry. Reading and diction.

ROSSETTI. Instead of a dowry. How does that work?

LIZZIE. He believes men with money have books. Therefore they seek wives who can read aloud. Because at the end of a hard day it is the wife's duty to provide her husband with entertainment.

ROSSETTI. Extraordinary piece of reasoning. Is his strategy working?

LIZZIE. Not so far... What kind of pictures do you paint? Hunt mentioned a Virgin Mary.

ROSSETTI. I have two Virgin Marys.

LIZZIE. Two?

ROSSETTI. Yes. My first was *The Girlhood of the Virgin Mary*, which sold for eighty pounds to Lady Bath. She's a friend of my aunt.

LIZZIE. Congratulations.

ROSSETTI. But then, even better, I painted *The Annunciation*.

LIZZIE. Did that sell?

ROSSETTI. Not yet. I offered it to Lady Bath. She said the Virgin looked alarmed. Well, if you were woken in bed in the middle of the night by a large angel, wouldn't you look alarmed?

LIZZIE. Yes, I think I would. Though I imagine I'd feel reassured once I'd seen the angel's wings.

ROSSETTI. He didn't have wings.

LIZZIE. No wings?

ROSSETTI. No.

LIZZIE. So she woke to find a large man in her bedroom?

ROSSETTI. He was obviously an angel, there were flames around his feet.

LIZZIE. His feet were on fire?

ROSSETTI. He was an angel.

LIZZIE. Of course he was.

ROSSETTI. Are you sure you're a seamstress and not a critic?

LIZZIE. I didn't mean to be critical. I think to be an artist must be very difficult and also wonderful.

ROSSETTI. It is difficult. And also, wonderful. I have an idea for a picture. I had it the day we met. The picture is called *Love at First Sight*.

LIZZIE. What would that look like?

ROSSETTI. I can demonstrate. Stay still for me.

LIZZIE *stops moving*.

Stillness is part of a picture's power. Real life is never still. Even now, you, even now, standing like you are, you think you are still, you are not. Your chest rises and falls with each breath. If I come close, I can see there is a vein, in your neck, moving.

LIZZIE. Perhaps you shouldn't come so close.

ROSSETTI. An artist must study his subject. My idea is that you are a princess. Do you have a handkerchief?

LIZZIE. No.

ROSSETTI. Take mine. (*Takes a handkerchief from his pocket and gives it to her.*) One day, you are passing by the royal stables, and your handkerchief falls to the ground...

She lets it fall.

But as you bend to retrieve it –

She bends.

– a stable groom reaches it first... (*Already on one knee, retrieving the handkerchief. Their faces almost meet.*) and he, looking up and seeing your face, falls in love.

Pause.

MILLAIS (*off*). Any chance of a cup of tea?

MILLAIS *enters, age twenty-two, smiley, breezy.*

ROSSETTI. Johnnie.

MILLAIS. Hello.

ROSSETTI. What are you doing here?

MILLAIS. I thought I'd come and get a cup of tea.

ROSSETTI. That's absurd. No one makes tea in the mornings – it's uncivilised. What do you want? I'm busy. Miss Siddal, Mr Millais – Mr Millais, / Miss Siddal.

MILLAIS. Miss Siddal, a pleasure to see you again.

LIZZIE. How do you do, Mr / Millais.

ROSSETTI. 'Again'?

MILLAIS. We met a month ago. Do you remember, Miss Siddal? I sketched you.

LIZZIE. Yes. /

ROSSETTI. You sketched her? Why?

MILLAIS. I liked her face.

ROSSETTI. When did she sit for you?

MILLAIS. She didn't. She was sitting for Hunt. I happened to call.

ROSSETTI. And sketched her?

MILLAIS. As an aide memoire.

ROSSETTI. What for?

MILLAIS. Faces are useful, aren't they. And, you know me, I like to have a pencil busy. How are you, Miss Siddal?

LIZZIE. I am well, thank you, sir.

MILLAIS. Excellent. No chance of tea?

ROSSETTI. If people guzzled tea in the morning, what would they do in the afternoon? Would you have breakfast at midnight? Should the Moon come up at midday?

MILLAIS. Just a cup of tea.

ROSSETTI. No. I'd come back in and find you halfway through a masterpiece. Miss Siddal is mine for the day and I won't have you drawing her better than me.

MILLAIS. Does the bonnet season start again soon, Miss Siddal?

LIZZIE. This very week.

MILLAIS. And ends in December, I believe?

LIZZIE. Yes.

ROSSETTI. You are very well informed about ladies' headgear.

MILLAIS. Yes I am.

LIZZIE. How is your picture, Mr Millais? Of Jesus as a boy.

MILLAIS. You remembered. Yes, it's done.

ROSSETTI. It is brilliant, dammit.

MILLAIS. Thank you. (*To* LIZZIE.) I've painted a real boy, in a real carpenter's shop. But rendered simply, as if straight from the heart. Like in the early Renaissance, when truth and feeling carried the day. The Academy will hate it.

LIZZIE. Then how brave of you to do it.

ROSSETTI *scowls*. MILLAIS *notices*.

MILLAIS. But Gabriel is a good painter. When he finds the time. I suppose it's difficult to write *and* paint. Have you done much writing lately?

ROSSETTI. I may have done.

MILLAIS. I'd love to hear some.

ROSSETTI. I'm drawing.

MILLAIS. Of course. Anyway, it's Miss Siddal I came to see. Mr Hunt told me you were coming here, Miss Siddal. I wonder, might I have a word?

ROSSETTI. Now? She's working.

MILLAIS. Gabriel, you spent half last winter in my studio, chattering away.

ROSSETTI. I don't remember that.

MILLAIS. And you were very welcome – as surely I am now. Don't let me stop you. Pick up your pencil. I'm not here.

ROSSETTI *picks up a pencil and drawing board and sits, with bad grace. He starts to sketch.*

Miss Siddal. I have spent all summer on a riverbank, studying, sketching – reeds and flowers and leaves…

ROSSETTI (*yawns*). Sorry. Tired.

MILLAIS. These weeks of preparation were for a subject I have long cherished.

ROSSETTI. Which one?

MILLAIS. I am coming to it. (*To* LIZZIE.) A young woman is brutally jilted by a prince. This self-same prince then stabs and murders her father. She loses her mind. Weighed down with grief, she climbs upon a willow tree; the branch she climbs on breaks; she falls into the stream beneath.

ROSSETTI.
                    'Her clothes spread wide
      And mermaid-like / awhile they bore her up.'

LIZZIE.
                    – 'awhile they bore her up.'

Ophelia? Am I to be Ophelia?

MILLAIS. Would you?

ROSSETTI (*to* MILLAIS). Wait, wait, wait. You can't.

MILLAIS. I have it planned.

ROSSETTI. You can't put her in the stream.

MILLAIS. There is a better way / than that.

ROSSETTI. Is there? Is there? You paint from life.

MILLAIS. Of course / I do.

ROSSETTI. How would you put Lizzie in water?

MILLAIS. Exactly. That's the problem. And in January.

ROSSETTI. January?

MILLAIS. I have a bath.

ROSSETTI. No.

MILLAIS. Hear me out. I have a bath, Lizzie, a zinc bath which I intend to put on trestles.

ROSSETTI. Trestles?

MILLAIS. I'd fill the bath with water, then heat it from below with oil lamps.

ROSSETTI. Like a fish kettle.

MILLAIS. No, not like a fish kettle. The temperature would be just so.

ROSSETTI. The answer's no.

MILLAIS. I'm not asking / *you*.

ROSSETTI. Don't do it, Lizzie.

MILLAIS. Gabriel, what is going on?

LIZZIE (*gently*). Gabriel… (*To* MILLAIS.) How long would I have to stay in water?

MILLAIS. The detail must be dazzling. The technique is called painting on a white wet ground.

ROSSETTI. That would take weeks.

MILLAIS. Lizzie, you cannot conceive what this painting will be. I am, I think, the best painter in England. This will be my masterpiece. You will be Ophelia. Will you do it? Because if you will, I promise, I will make you immortal.

LIZZIE. Yes. Yes please.

ROSSETTI *gets up violently.*

MILLAIS. Is something the matter?

ROSSETTI. It's wrong.

MILLAIS. What is?

ROSSETTI. To paint her in water in winter.

MILLAIS. It'll be safe.

ROSSETTI. How will it be safe?

MILLAIS. I'll make sure it's / safe.

ROSSETTI. You will make sure it's safe?

MILLAIS. Yes, I will.

ROSSETTI. Who made the boy Jesus cry?

MILLAIS. I didn't make him cry; he cried.

ROSSETTI. Why did he cry?

MILLAIS. He got cramp.

ROSSETTI. Of course he got cramp! You wouldn't let him move!

MILLAIS. What's that got to do with *Ophelia*?

ROSSETTI. If you can reduce Jesus to tears, what are you going to do to an innocent woman?

MILLAIS. Nothing! And I fail to understand why you should be taking offence.

ROSSETTI. I think you should go. Please. You should. Go. You have disrupted my day.

Pause.

MILLAIS. So... I'll take my leave now, Miss Siddal. When the bonnet season is over, I shall be in communication. I cannot tell you how delighted I am.

LIZZIE. Thank you, sir.

MILLAIS. I don't want bad blood between us, Gabriel.

MILLAIS *proffers his hand.* ROSSETTI *folds his arms in response. A beat, then* MILLAIS *leaves.*

ROSSETTI. You cannot do it... Obviously you can if you want – but you can't possibly.

LIZZIE. Why shouldn't I?

ROSSETTI. Give up weeks of your life to pose in water? /

LIZZIE. You said yourself he's brilliant.

ROSSETTI. I may have said that.

LIZZIE. Then why shouldn't I pose for him? /

ROSSETTI. You're flattered. I can see you're flattered, you *are* flattered.

LIZZIE. And if I am?

ROSSETTI. And now you'll drown. Or freeze. Or the oil lamps will catch your dress on fire and you'll end up scarred for the rest of / your days.

LIZZIE. Gabriel, Gabriel, he won't harm me. He's an artist.

ROSSETTI. *You cannot trust an artist!* I mean, obviously you *can* trust an artist, except there are times when you *can't.* An artist is judged on his picture, not on the damage he causes in making it. He'll do what he must, to get what he wants. He won't care about you.

LIZZIE. Why would he care about *me*? I'm a model.

ROSSETTI. Well, he should care. Look at you, you're lovely, you should be cared for – somebody should – I mean, why not? – we should all care about each other. Jesus said that, I think – something like it. I'm so agitated, I have lost all eloquence.

Pause.

LIZZIE (*gently*). It must be hard for you to understand. Your life is teeming with events – you create them. The rest of us – in our lives – nothing happens from week to week. We are drudges. One day we'll die and it will be as if we never lived.

ROSSETTI. How will that be altered by lying in a bath?

LIZZIE. Something of me will be in his painting. Something of me will be worth poetry and tears. Or perhaps you consider me too ordinary to be a heroine. You may / be right.

ROSSETTI. I haven't said / that.

LIZZIE. You're entitled to your opinion, but it is not / the opinion of Mr Millais.

ROSSETTI. It is not my opinion. I did not / say any such thing

LIZZIE. Nor Mr Deverell, either.

ROSSETTI. Mr – ? *Walter* Deverell?

LIZZIE. Yes. Walter Deverell. The artist. I was Viola. In his painting of *Twelfth Night*.

ROSSETTI. That was your face?

LIZZIE. Yes.

ROSSETTI. Was it?… Walter is very good with trees.

LIZZIE. Yes, his trees are excellent.

ROSSETTI. He's not so good with…

LIZZIE.…faces, no. (*It's a truce.*) I think I draw as well as he does. And I've only just begun.

ROSSETTI. Begun?

LIZZIE. To draw.

ROSSETTI. You draw?

LIZZIE. It's a new law they've brought in – even common girls are now allowed to purchase pencils if they can save up thruppence.

ROSSETTI. You are not common. You are not. You are the most
rare creature. (*A thought occurs*.) I can teach you. I can teach
you. To draw, to paint. I can teach you everything I know.

LIZZIE. Why would you do that?

ROSSETTI. Because the day I met you, I came back here and
wrote a poem straight away. Would you care to hear it?

LIZZIE. Yes.

ROSSETTI....
'I have been here before,
But when or how I cannot tell:
I know the grass beyond the door,
The sweet keen smell,
The sighing sound, the lights around the shore.

You have been mine before,
How long ago I may not know:
But just when at that swallow's soar
Your neck turned so,
Some veil did fall – I knew it all of yore.

Then, now, – perchance again!...
O round mine eyes your tresses shake!
Shall we not lie as we have lain
Thus for Love's sake,
And sleep, and wake, yet never break the chain?'

...Let me teach you about art.

A clap of thunder ushers in the next scene.

Scene Four

Autumn. Parkland in Kent.

Steady rain is falling. HUNT *sits on a stool, drawing, under an umbrella held by* MILLAIS. HUNT *is oblivious to the weather and to* MILLAIS, *who has an artist's bag on his shoulder.*

MILLAIS. Maniac.

HUNT. Yes?

MILLAIS. It's still raining.

HUNT. Yes.

MILLAIS. We could move in under those trees.

HUNT. That might disturb the deer. If they run away, I'd have to start again.

MILLAIS. But I can't use my watercolours in the rain.

HUNT. Obviously not.

MILLAIS. And I can't work at all if I'm holding the umbrella.

HUNT. No.

MILLAIS. And my arm's getting tired.

HUNT. Is it? Uh-huh. No, the thing is, she's a whore. Well, I wasn't surprised – most models are whores. But that doesn't mean I shouldn't consider… you know… Jesus saved whores, didn't he. He went round Galilee saving whores.

MILLAIS. I don't think that was his primary purpose.

HUNT. I mean, I'm not saying I'm going to marry her. But suppose one could civilise her. Do you think it's possible to elevate a woman through rigorous education and immersion in the arts?

MILLAIS. No.

HUNT. Literature is full of maids who are rescued by knights and become ladies.

MILLAIS. Yes, it's called fiction. Written by men who can't attract women.

HUNT. I think reclaiming a woman would be a heroic act. Mind – you'd have to invent a past – you couldn't tell the truth. Imagine taking her home to meet your parents. 'This is my intended. She used to be a model.' You'd have to bring both parents round with smelling salts.

MILLAIS. Actually, not all models are whores.

HUNT. Most of them are – always have been. The galleries of England are festooned with trollops. You can walk into any aristocrat's home and the proud owner will point to his wall and say 'Look at my Venus' or 'Have you seen my Boudicca?', and you look up and there's some tart staring down at you.

MILLAIS. What's her name? This woman you want to save?

HUNT. I'm not saying I'm going to. Annie Miller. Gabriel knows her.

MILLAIS. I haven't spoken to Gabriel in a month.

HUNT. Nor have I. I wish he was here. He's cheerful.

MILLAIS. I'm sure he's cheerful. He's nice and dry in Highgate.

Scene Five

ROSSETTI *arranging chairs and an easel in his studio in Highgate. He hears someone coming.*

ROSSETTI. Hello? Lizzie?

HUNT (*off*). Hullo?… Hullo?

HUNT *enters.*

Gabriel. Lord, how it rained in Kent. I nearly rounded up the animals and built an ark.

ROSSETTI. What are you doing here?

HUNT. I was on my way to meet Brown. Thought I'd call in here and see if you'd died. Have you died?

ROSSETTI. No.

HUNT. Good. What have you been up to?

ROSSETTI. Working.

HUNT. Really? Well done. On what?

ROSSETTI. Oh, drawings mostly.

HUNT. Drawings? What drawings?

ROSSETTI. Oh, just – you know – whatever I could see around me.

HUNT. Can I look?

ROSSETTI. Well.

> HUNT *is already picking up* ROSSETTI's *drawings and sifting through them.*

HUNT. My God, wonderful. Very fine. This looks like Lizzie Siddal.

ROSSETTI. Does it?

HUNT. So does this… And this… They all look like Lizzie Siddal.

ROSSETTI. Do they?

HUNT. You know they do. There's got to be several weeks' work. Why have you kept drawing her?

ROSSETTI. No reason. She must have just popped into my head.

> LIZZIE *enters and taps on the door to announce her arrival. She has a wooden watercolour field box and a drawing book.*

LIZZIE. Good morning, Mr Hunt.

HUNT. Lizzie.

LIZZIE. How pleasant to see you.

HUNT. What are you doing here? – That's my field box. /

ROSSETTI (*softly*). Oh, Christ. /

HUNT. Isn't it? Yes, that's my mark. That's my field box – the one I lent you at Knole Park. (*Indicating the box.*) May I?

LIZZIE. Yes, of course.

She hands HUNT *the box.*

HUNT. Yes. This is mine. /

ROSSETTI (*to* LIZZIE). I'll buy you another. /

LIZZIE. There's no need. /

ROSSETTI. I will. /

HUNT. What's she doing with my field box?

ROSSETTI. I gave it to her.

HUNT. It's not yours to give.

ROSSETTI. She didn't have one.

HUNT. Why give her mine?

ROSSETTI. To paint with.

HUNT. Oh Lord, I hope you haven't ruined my paints.

LIZZIE. No, I / haven't.

HUNT. The last box I had was ruined by my niece.

ROSSETTI. Lizzie's not a child.

HUNT. No, but she's not an artist either.

LIZZIE. I am. I am now… I am become one.

HUNT.…What does that mean?

LIZZIE. I am become an artist.

HUNT. You're a seamstress.

LIZZIE. I left.

HUNT. You left your job?

LIZZIE. To be an artist, yes.

HUNT. Good God, why?

LIZZIE. To commit to art. All or nothing.

ROSSETTI. The only way to be.

HUNT. That's nonsense.

ROSSETTI. No it isn't.

HUNT. Of course it is. Anyone can't suddenly up and be an artist.

ROSSETTI. Why not?

HUNT. You know why not. Artists are born with talent, given of God.

ROSSETTI. Lizzie has talent.

HUNT. Does she? (*To* LIZZIE.) Do you? Where's the evidence?

LIZZIE (*tightening her grip on her folder*). Well, I've only just begun.

HUNT. Where have you studied?

LIZZIE. I haven't.

HUNT. Do you have ambitions? Precepts? What do you hope to accomplish?

LIZZIE. 'To accomplish'?

HUNT. I hope to teach the world to behave better through the moral force of my images. What do you hope to do?

LIZZIE. I don't know.

ROSSETTI. We don't want to teach anyone how to behave.

HUNT. 'We'?

ROSSETTI. Lizzie is my pupil.

A beat. HUNT *catches up.*

HUNT. Well, there's a thing. Brave new world. How will you eat?

LIZZIE. At my parents' table.

HUNT. Without bringing home wages?

LIZZIE. I am modelling for Millais soon. They can have the fee.

HUNT. And after that?

LIZZIE. I will sell my pictures.

HUNT. Will you? Mm-hm. Good Lord, I've only just realised how late I am. Please accept this as a small gift. May it bring you joy.

He hands back the box.

LIZZIE. Mr Hunt...

HUNT. Holman. Call me Holman. No need to thank me. Fellow artist. Why not?

(*A nod of farewell to* ROSSETTI.) Gabriel. Forgive me. I'd like to stay and spoil your day, but Brown sulks if I'm late. See you some time.

HUNT *goes.*

ROSSETTI. Yes. Give my regards to Brown. (*To* LIZZIE.) That man really is the most contrary / fellow.

LIZZIE. He gave me his paints.

ROSSETTI. Yes, that was kind.

LIZZIE. So generous of him. And of *you* to give me his paints before *he* did.

ROSSETTI. I'm sorry. I'd forgotten they were his. I do think you might have shown him your drawings. He'd have seen your genius.

LIZZIE. I have no genius, / Gabriel.

ROSSETTI. You are absolutely the / most gifted...

LIZZIE. Please, don't over-praise me. /

ROSSETTI. I cannot over-praise you. You are beyond my powers of / praise.

LIZZIE. No. No, no, no. No. You must stop this.

ROSSETTI. How can I stop? How? I am caught. Every day I am stuck. I am bound. Spellbound. Spending the day within touching distance. Not that I would.

LIZZIE. I cannot come here every day if I am under siege.

ROSSETTI. You are not.

LIZZIE. My mother's convinced my castle walls have already fallen.

ROSSETTI. I shall write to your mother and tell her you could not be safer if you were in a convent. And I know, even if I tried to touch that hand... just touch it... that you would deny me.

He is reaching out.

LIZZIE. Yes, I would.

He withdraws his hand. LIZZIE picks up a pencil and opens her drawing book.

ROSSETTI. I had not suspected you could be so cold. And here am I, your poor, pitiful, penniless poet. Left to languish, lovelorn. Without a word of comfort.

LIZZIE. I had thought you better than this.

ROSSETTI. In what way better? Is there a better way to be than loving / you?

LIZZIE. You don't mean what you say. /

ROSSETTI. I mean every word.

LIZZIE. You say you are penniless, but you are rich in words. You spend them all day long. They cost you nothing and they mean nothing, but if I were to believe them once, think what they might cost me.

ROSSETTI. What might they cost you?

LIZZIE. You are a man.

ROSSETTI. Yes?

LIZZIE. My father used to say, 'Beware young men. They wish to enjoy the fruit. Without owning the tree.'

ROSSETTI. What does that mean?

LIZZIE. I wonder.

ROSSETTI. You are a holy thing to me.

LIZZIE. You cannot say what isn't true.

ROSSETTI. It is true. But if you say I cannot say it, then I won't. Your wish is my command.

LIZZIE. Is it?

ROSSETTI. Yes.

LIZZIE. My wish is your command?

ROSSETTI. Yes.

LIZZIE. In that case, sit for me.

ROSSETTI. Nooooh.

LIZZIE. Yes. Yes. You said one day you'd sit for me. It is my wish. Sit for me. Will you? Would you?

LIZZIE *waits*. ROSSETTI *sits and folds his arms. She smiles*.

Thank you.

She starts to draw.

ROSSETTI. God, I hate this. I hate being a model. It makes me feel like an object.

LIZZIE. You *are* an object. Sit still while I draw.

ROSSETTI. How did this happen? I was enjoying myself and then... Don't just draw me as I am. Make me some personage. St George.

LIZZIE. St George was a warrior.

ROSSETTI. I could be a warrior.

LIZZIE. You're a poet.

ROSSETTI. Poets are tough. Don't underestimate poets.

LIZZIE. You're so right. Wasn't it the Duke of Wellington at Waterloo who said, 'There is only one thing that can save us now. Send in the battalion of poets.'

ROSSETTI. ... I would fight for *you*. I adore you. When you're here I'm alive, when you're gone, I'm a dead man. I sit bereft of life and wonder what you're doing – who you're with. Are they making you laugh? I want you to laugh, but I don't want anyone else to make you laugh. I want it to be me. Do you think of me? Say something.

LIZZIE. What would you have me say?

ROSSETTI. Tell me the truth.

LIZZIE. You are a god of painting. A prince of poets. And a
man of charm. You could talk your way into the Underworld
and out again. Any woman in Christendom would be glad of
a greeting from you – would store your words in her heart
for ever – would stitch her soul to yours if she could. I have
never met anyone like you, nor hoped to meet anyone like
you... Now sit still. Let me finish my drawing.

She draws.

Scene Six

Dusk. The Royal Academy's Summer Exhibition.

MILLAIS *stands admiring his own painting of* Ophelia. JOHN
RUSKIN *appears and stops some distance away. He's in his
early thirties.*

MILLAIS. Mr Ruskin.

RUSKIN. Man never tires of looking at beauty. Have you
created beauty, Johnnie?

MILLAIS. You have not seen it yet?

RUSKIN. I have been in Venice. Effie and I arrived back
yesterday.

MILLAIS. How is your wife?

RUSKIN. She is well. They're taking it down tonight, I gather.

MILLAIS. In the next half-hour.

RUSKIN. I hear there never was such pushing and shoving
round a painting. I asked the Academy if I could slip in after
hours. They said yes.

MILLAIS. The critics were their normal sniffy selves.

RUSKIN. I'm a critic.

MILLAIS. You're not going to be sniffy, are you, sir?

RUSKIN. I might be. Shall I take a look?

RUSKIN *studies the painting.*

At the same time, in an apartment in Blackfriars, it is also dusk.

ROSSETTI *is there, waiting for* LIZZIE, *who comes in, brimming with excitement.*

LIZZIE. I'm so sorry, Gabriel.

ROSSETTI. It's all right. Really.

LIZZIE. I had to queue.

ROSSETTI. Did you?

LIZZIE. There was a crowd round the painting. The attendant kept saying 'move along' but no one moved. And I was standing there and a woman looked at me and said, 'It's her.' And then people were turning round and *I* was the centre of attention. And an old man with a wig said I was better than the painting, and then a little blond boy said the painting was beautiful but I was ugly, and his mother smacked him, and then blond boy started crying and people were laughing, and the attendant told everyone to be quiet, and wanted to know what the fuss was. And he asked if it really was me in the picture and I said yes. And then he cleared a space, and let me stand there on my own, for two whole minutes, and look. And everyone was quiet. And then I said thank you, and then I turned to go and there was applause. For me. There was applause.

ROSSETTI. Really.

LIZZIE. I am Ophelia.

ROSSETTI. Yes.

LIZZIE. Are you not thrilled for me?

ROSSETTI. Of course I am. I am, yes. Yes. I have been waiting for an hour, that's all.

LIZZIE. I'm so sorry.

ROSSETTI. No, I'm sorry. I… I don't mean to be unenthusiastic.

LIZZIE. Of course you don't. An hour. How annoying.

ROSSETTI. It's all right. Really. I am glad for you. What a tremendous success.

LIZZIE. It's Millais' success.

ROSSETTI. Yes. I loathe his success. I loathe him. He made you ill.

LIZZIE. I'm better now. And this. (*Gesturing at the room.*) You're renting this?

ROSSETTI. With William, yes.

LIZZIE. It's spectacular.

ROSSETTI. There's a view of the Thames. From my bedroom.

LIZZIE. How wonderful. Where *is* your brother?

ROSSETTI. He's staying the night at my mother's.

LIZZIE. Is he?

ROSSETTI. I thought we could do some painting together. And I bought you a gift. (*Searches his pockets.*) It's in my coat. Wait.

He goes. She waits.

In the Academy, RUSKIN *speaks at last.*

RUSKIN. My boy, it is, I have to tell you, exquisite.

MILLAIS. Thank you.

RUSKIN. And yet…

MILLAIS. And yet?

RUSKIN. No. No, no, it's lovely. And yet…

MILLAIS. And yet?

ROSSETTI. There's something troubling me. There's something wrong with it.

In the apartment, ROSSETTI *returns with something tiny in his hand.*

LIZZIE. What is it?

He reveals a solid 'cake' or pan of watercolour wrapped in foil.

ROSSETTI. Dragon's Blood. A two-shilling cake.

LIZZIE *takes it.*

LIZZIE (*chuckles*). Oh, Gabriel. Shall I paint in Dragon's Blood? Did you kill a dragon for me?

ROSSETTI. Of course I did.

LIZZIE. Where's the head?

ROSSETTI. I threw it in the river.

LIZZIE. I'd like to see the river.

ROSSETTI. Would you? Well, you could see it from my bedroom. If you'd like to.

They kiss. Then surface. Then exit.

In the Academy, RUSKIN *speaks again.*

RUSKIN. Who is the model?

MILLAIS. Elizabeth Siddal. Hunt painted her before me.

RUSKIN. Did he?

MILLAIS. 'And yet.' You said 'and yet'.

RUSKIN. The shadows are wrong. You've made them too cold.

MILLAIS. I don't think so.

RUSKIN. Yes. You have. I thought the whole point of you Pre-Raphaelites is that you render the truth and nothing but the truth. And her skin. You've used some rather crude purples and yellows. I suppose you mean to suggest transparency on the skin.

MILLAIS. She's dying, John.

RUSKIN. Yes, but the effect is too melancholy to be true. You have embellished instead of painting what you saw.

MILLAIS. I painted what I saw.

RUSKIN. There's an excess of tragedy in the girl.

MILLAIS. Yes. That's what I saw.

Scene Seven

Six months later. The beach at Hastings. A bright April morning. The sound of seagulls and the sea on shingle.

ROSSETTI *is coming up the beach with a beaker of seawater.* LIZZIE *waits. Both of them are in good spirits.*

ROSSETTI. You will drink this. You must. I have braved sea monsters to get it.

LIZZIE. Where are the sea monsters?

ROSSETTI. They're just below the surface. I could have been dragged in at any moment. Worth it though because – mmm – if I'm not mistaken this is Hastings seawater – recommended by doctors – fresh, tangy, salty.

LIZZIE. Is that the same water that fish float in, and poor drowned sailors? And do passing ships empty their bilge pumps into it?

ROSSETTI. It will do you good.

LIZZIE. I don't think it will.

ROSSETTI. Then why do doctors recommend it?

LIZZIE. Doctors recommend it; they don't drink it. Doctors drink claret.

ROSSETTI. I could sell this in the Strand for a guinea.

LIZZIE. Then you should fill a bucket and take it on the train to London tomorrow.

ROSSETTI. I do think you might be more obliging. I pawned my dead father's gold pin to pay for our lodgings.

LIZZIE. Your father's spirit kisses you for doing so.

ROSSETTI. The whole point of Hastings is to make people healthy. Otherwise what is the point of Hastings?

LIZZIE. I am healthy.

ROSSETTI. Healthy people don't get chest infections that last all winter.

LIZZIE. It's disappeared now. I could come back on the train with you.

ROSSETTI. No. I've paid for your room for another week.

LIZZIE. Why would I want to stay on here if you're in London?

ROSSETTI. Better if you stay. We wouldn't see each other in London anyway. I have pictures to finish; people to see; a sponsor I have to charm.

LIZZIE. You don't want me there.

ROSSETTI. I want you healthy. Stay here.

LIZZIE. I wouldn't distract you. I could stand in the street outside. You could look out of your window from time to time. I'd see your face.

ROSSETTI. Halfwit.

LIZZIE. Ninny.

ROSSETTI. Goose.

LIZZIE. Booby.

ROSSETTI. Featherbrain.

LIZZIE. Oaf.

ROSSETTI. Whey-face.

LIZZIE. Thank you for the holiday.

ROSSETTI. My absolute pleasure. When I have money, we'll have holidays all the time. We are artists. We must have a surfeit of everything. We cannot live ordinary lives. That would be a crime.

LIZZIE. Is it a crime to be ordinary?

ROSSETTI. Yes. An artist must go beyond the pale. How else could we encompass the passions we are supposed to represent? How could you write *Romeo and Juliet* if all you knew was the plough and the field, and the daily plod? If all you did was scratch ink in an office, how could you paint Lancelot trapped in the Queen's chamber? We lead large lives so that we feel able to write them and paint them. Hero, Leander, Romeo, Juliet, Dante, Beatrice. All the great loves.

LIZZIE.... All the great loves died young. Leander drowns and Hero kills herself. Romeo thinks Juliet dead and so he kills himself. And then she kills herself. And Dante loves Beatrice, who dies at twenty and then he pines.

ROSSETTI. Yes.

LIZZIE. Then do we have to die young?

ROSSETTI. Us? No.

LIZZIE. But ours is a great love, too.

ROSSETTI. It is.

LIZZIE. Then I'll have to drown myself.

ROSSETTI. You have no reason to drown yourself.

LIZZIE. I have every reason. I am a fallen woman. Worse – my lover abandons me tomorrow for London. There he will probably visit his mother. What she looks like I do not know, for I have never met her.

A beat.

ROSSETTI. I will invite you to meet my mother the moment you get back.

LIZZIE. You will?

ROSSETTI. I will.

LIZZIE. Gabriel! You promise?

ROSSETTI. I do.

She starts to embrace him.

LIZZIE. Oh, Gabriel! /

ROSSETTI. Lizzie, Lizzie, we're in public.

LIZZIE. It's all right. I'm an artist.

She kisses him on the cheek. ROSSETTI *looks around.*

...How can a poet be so prim?

ROSSETTI. I am not prim. I am not prim.

LIZZIE. Spoken by the man who doesn't dare come to my room at night.

ROSSETTI. I cannot come to your room. The landlady is a dragon in human form. She stalks the corridors.

LIZZIE. You slay dragons.

ROSSETTI. I think I may have mentioned the creaky floorboards between your room and mine.

LIZZIE. 'An artist must go beyond the pale.'

ROSSETTI. What would you have me do?

LIZZIE. There's an ironmonger's in Trinity Street. I would have you go there and buy French chalk.

ROSSETTI. Why would I want French chalk?

LIZZIE. Because you are not prim. Because you are bold and dashing. Because you are the great Dante Gabriel Rossetti, and when you puff French chalk between floorboards, they don't creak.

The sound of the sea swells. Waves crash resoundingly as if sweeping all away and then fade, replaced by the sounds of a London street in the 1850s.

Scene Eight

It is three years later. ROSSETTI's *apartment. A spring afternoon. Chairs. An easel. A small table.*

LIZZIE *sits and begins to draw with great concentration.* ROSSETTI *enters.*

ROSSETTI. What are you doing now?

LIZZIE. Darkening the hair.

ROSSETTI. Not now. Don't change what he's seen.

LIZZIE. But if I can do it better.

ROSSETTI. No, no, he's coming. We should be ready…

LIZZIE *puts her drawing and pencil to one side.*

And happy.

Pause.

You won't give the impression that you're too familiar with the apartment?

LIZZIE. No.

ROSSETTI. I don't want Ruskin to think you live here.

LIZZIE. I don't live here.

ROSSETTI. Or spend the night.

LIZZIE. I don't. I haven't. Not for a long time.

ROSSETTI. It's just that he thinks you're my pupil. I wouldn't want him to think other thoughts.

LIZZIE. You can call your brother to give evidence.

ROSSETTI. William's not back till late. He's going round to Charlotte Street.

LIZZIE.…How *is* your dear mother? Her nerves – are they better?

ROSSETTI. A little.

LIZZIE. But still not strong enough to cope with meeting me?

ROSSETTI. Soon.

LIZZIE. Really?

ROSSETTI. Yes.

LIZZIE. Such a will o' the wisp, your mother. So hard to pin down. Always off 'visiting cousins', or 'busy this week', or 'not very well'. Three years she's been doing that now. /

ROSSETTI. It's not three years. /

LIZZIE. Three years since you stood on a beach in Hastings and promised you'd introduce me.

ROSSETTI. I am about to introduce you to the greatest critic of the age: John Ruskin.

LIZZIE. But not your mother.

ROSSETTI. Can we just concentrate on Ruskin? Can we? For now? And then later, after, we can talk about other things, yes?

LIZZIE.…No.

ROSSETTI. What?

LIZZIE. No, no. I'm sorry, no – we can't. We can't. I'm sorry, I have a question, it's urgent, I'm so sorry, Gabriel, but I ask myself this question every night before I go to sleep. And when I wake in the morning the question is still there. I carry the question in my head all the time. All the time.

ROSSETTI. Very well. What is the question?

LIZZIE. Do you grow tired of me, Gabriel?

ROSSETTI.…No.

LIZZIE.…Are you sure?… Possession makes some men weary. I wonder if you are weary.

ROSSETTI. I'm not. I don't know how you can ask that. How can you ask that?

LIZZIE. Because. Because I feel that Love should not hesitate. And you do. (*Indicating drawings and paintings*.) In your pictures, Love plunges in, Love cannot help itself – it leaps like Leander into the sea. Love makes love – and is damned like Paolo and Francesca. Love is Lancelot – torn by guilt, but loving anyway. I wonder why you hang back.

ROSSETTI. I do not hang back. I never hang back. I do not hesitate in anything.

LIZZIE. Is it consequence you shy away from? The consequence of love might be a child. Is that the cause?

ROSSETTI. This is not to be believed. That you should broach this now. I am about to bring you Ruskin and you speak of intimacies? The subject of the bedroom should stay in the bedroom.

LIZZIE. But we are never *in* the bedroom.

The sound of a door knocker.

ROSSETTI. Where's your folder?

LIZZIE. I'll get it.

LIZZIE exits. ROSSETTI goes to the door.

HUNT enters with ANNIE MILLER – in her early twenties.

HUNT. Sorry to barge in. How are you? You know Annie.

ANNIE. 'Allo / Gabriel.

HUNT. Is this convenient?

ANNIE. 'Ow are / ya?

ROSSETTI. No. No, it's not convenient.

HUNT. Isn't it? Why isn't it convenient?

ROSSETTI. I'm expecting Ruskin.

HUNT. Ruskin?

ROSSETTI. You can't stay. He'll be here soon. (*Big smile.*) Hello, Annie. You are a stunner.

ANNIE. Am I? I like your apartment. Ain't you a swell.

HUNT. His brother lives here too – William – he pays the rent.

ROSSETTI. No he doesn't.

HUNT. He works at the Inland Revenue. They're never short of a shilling.

ROSSETTI. I also pay rent. Some of the rent. Some of the time.

HUNT. Are you getting commissions from Ruskin now?

ROSSETTI. I am.

HUNT. I thought you'd nip in there.

ROSSETTI. I didn't nip in. He needed a protégé.

HUNT. And you were passing.

ROSSETTI. What is it you want?

HUNT. Dammit, Gabriel, I want our friendship back. I want our youth back. I want to row down the Thames in the morning mist, do you remember?

ROSSETTI. Yes. Strenuous way to start the day.

HUNT. Not for you – you didn't do any rowing – *I* did all the rowing. You spouted poetry to uncomprehending ducks.

ROSSETTI. They were not uncomprehending. They were particularly appreciative of 'The Blessed Damozel'.

HUNT. 'The blessed Damozel leaned out...'

ROSSETTI.
> '...From the gold bar of Heaven;
> Her eyes were deeper than the depth
> Of waters stilled at even;
> She had three lilies in her hand,
> And the stars in her hair were seven.'

HUNT quacks like a flock of appreciative ducks. LIZZIE returns, carrying an art folder. HUNT stops quacking.

HUNT. Lizzie. Are you living here now?

LIZZIE. No, of course I'm not.

HUNT. Oh. Well, anyway, how are you? May I present Annie Miller? Annie, this is Lizzie Siddal, Gabriel's special friend.

ANNIE. Pleasure to meet you, I'm sure.

LIZZIE (*friendly*). How do you do.

ANNIE. I know oo you are.

LIZZIE. Do you?

ANNIE. You're the one nearly drowned in the painting.

HUNT. *Ophelia*.

ANNIE. That's the one, the one you nearly drowned for.

HUNT. She didn't drown.

ANNIE. She did nearly.

HUNT. She didn't drown. She nearly froze. The lamps heating the bath went out. She nearly froze.

ANNIE. All right, all right, don't kick up a shine, I'm only talkin'.

HUNT. We're in company.

ANNIE. I can see we're in comp'ny. I can see – the – comp'ny. They're in front of me.

LIZZIE. I've recovered now though so all is well.

HUNT. She got pneumonia.

ANNIE. Noomonia? 'Ow come?

HUNT (*exasperated*). The water in the bath was cold!

ANNIE. Well, why didn't she get out the bath? (*To* LIZZIE.) Why didn't you get out the bath?

LIZZIE. It would have disturbed the artist.

ANNIE *finds this absurd. The others don't. Short pause.*

It's best forgotten. We're expecting / Ruskin.

ROSSETTI. I've told / them.

HUNT. We won't stay, Liz, don't fret. Just five minutes, then we'll go.

ROSSETTI. It's Lizzie whom Ruskin is coming to see.

HUNT. Lizzie? What for?

LIZZIE. Gabriel showed Ruskin my pictures. Isn't that kind of him?

HUNT (*to* ROSSETTI). Why would you do that?

ROSSETTI. I thought he might like them.

HUNT. Which pictures? The kid in tears – that one?

LIZZIE. Do you mean the grieving child from Wordsworth's poem 'We Are Seven'?

HUNT. Yes, that one. And the sad women on the shore?

LIZZIE. It's called *The Ladies Lament*. From the ballad by Sir Patrick Spens.

HUNT. What did Ruskin say?

ROSSETTI. He liked her work.

HUNT. He didn't think it too naive?

ROSSETTI. No, he didn't.

HUNT. And now he wants to meet you?

LIZZIE. We hope he might buy something. Wouldn't that be extraordinary?

HUNT. Yes. It would. (*To* ROSSETTI.) Although, if he liked the work, why didn't he go ahead and buy it? Why does he need to meet her?

ROSSETTI. We don't know.

HUNT (*to* ANNIE). Lizzie draws and paints.

ANNIE. Oh.

HUNT. She's been under Gabriel's tutelage.

ANNIE. 'As she now? That sounds a bit filthy, if you ask / me.

HUNT (*suddenly incensed*). This is what I mean. This is where we fall / down.

ANNIE. What you sayin' / now?

HUNT. The simplest / conversation –

ANNIE. Don't start, Holman, don't you even / think of starting.

HUNT. You cannot join in unless you learn how to speak with / decorum.

ANNIE. I'm learnin' 'ow to speak, why don't you learn your / manners?

LIZZIE. Miss Miller… Forgive my interrupting. I wouldn't normally be so blunt. We're expecting an important visitor. I wonder could you come back another day? Tomorrow? Or Thursday?

ROSSETTI. Yes, perhaps the two of you could suspend your row till Thursday? We'd love to watch you fight then, wouldn't we, Lizzie? Do you have a row booked for Thursday? Could we fit one in?

HUNT. How very droll.

LIZZIE. Unless your business really is urgent in some way?

ANNIE. Oh, don't ask me, dearie, ask 'is / nibs.

HUNT. If I may speak a sentence un-heckled? There is one pressing matter. As you know, I am off to the Holy Land; I shall be gone several months. I am bent on creating a work there that will render all other painting this century second rate. However my absence is unfortunate in one regard: that Miss Miller and I have recently formed an attachment. It's difficult to believe, but there are times when Miss Miller can actually be a very pleasing companion.

ANNIE. Oh, can I?

HUNT. Will you shut up please?

ANNIE. I'm gonna go.

HUNT. Then go.

ANNIE. I need money for a cab.

HUNT. In a minute. While I'm away, I'm paying for Miss Miller to have lessons in how to be a lady. How to walk and

talk and sit. And cross her legs. She'll be going to a Mrs
Bramah in Cheyne Gardens – do you know her, Lizzie?

LIZZIE. No. Why would I?

HUNT. Well, you're more ladylike than some. I always
assumed you'd had lessons.

LIZZIE. No.

ROSSETTI. What do you want me to do, Maniac?

HUNT. I want to be clear. I have not promised to marry Miss
Miller. She is not fit currently to be a wife. However, if on
my return, I judge that she is fit, I may – or I may not – or
I / may –

ANNIE. Oh, for Gawd's sake, spit it / out.

HUNT. Will you be quiet?

ROSSETTI. You want me to keep an eye on her, is that it?

HUNT. Yes! Yes! Exactly that! This is a woman who thinks the
way to stave off temptation is to give in to it. Could you keep
an eye on her? Would you do that, Gabriel? Look after your
old friend's special friend?

ROSSETTI. It would be a pleasure.

ANNIE. You gonna paint me, Gabriel? While 'e's gone? You
gonna do me again?

ROSSETTI. Do you know, I'd like that very much.

ANNIE. Would ya now?

HUNT. And you, Lizzie. Perhaps I could ask you to keep an eye
on her too?

LIZZIE. Me?… No.

HUNT. No?

LIZZIE. No.

ANNIE. Charmed, I'm sure.

ROSSETTI. Liz.

LIZZIE (*to* HUNT). Are you going to Palestine? Take her with
you. If I was a man-loved-a-woman, I wouldn't want her
from my side for a moment. And if she truly loved you, the
ends of the earth would not be too far to follow. All you're
saying is, 'See this woman? I don't trust her. Watch her till I
come back.'

ANNIE (*to* HUNT). And you said *I* wasn't up to comp'ny.

HUNT (*to* LIZZIE). I am *staggered* at your / inference –

ROSSETTI. Maniac! Maniac. Maniac. It's all right, it's all
right. Friend. Friend... Come in the next room. I... I wanted
to show you *Dante's Vision of Rachel and Leah*.

HUNT....Right.

ROSSETTI (*to* LIZZIE). We'll only be a minute.

HUNT *and* ROSSETTI *exit. There's a pause.*

ANNIE.... 'E ain't married ya then?

LIZZIE. No.

ANNIE. Some do, some don't. Spec you're doin' all right
though. Bet you're flush. Did 'e buy you that dress?

LIZZIE. No. I made this dress.

ANNIE. Oh. But 'e does buy you things though, don't 'e. That's
how the world turns. You show 'im what's under your frock,
'e'll show you what's in 'is pocket. Bargain while you can, I
say. Cuz 'e ain't gonna be keen for ever. No man wants to
spend 'is whole life diggin' the same trench. It's 'ow they're
made. We all got to get out the gutter, some'ow, int we.

LIZZIE. I've never been in the gutter.

ANNIE. Lucky you. I was. Me, I never 'ad a mum. 'Ad a dad,
but 'e went soft in the 'ead. I was on the game at twelve. I'm
not ashamed. Tell *you*, I tell *everyone*. All I could do. I was
living with me aunt, but 'er 'usband started feeling me up.
Yeah.

LIZZIE. I'm so sorry.

ANNIE. Dirty bastard.

LIZZIE. How terrifying for you.

ANNIE. Dun't matter. It's only fingers. 'E was a cobbler. 'Is fingers was black. Left marks on me skin. It washes off. Not that I 'ardly washed then. I do now. Holman's particular in that way. 'E's a lunatic for baths. What's your Gabriel like? Is 'e like that?

LIZZIE. I'm sorry. I can't discuss that. I don't mean to be unfriendly.

ANNIE. Go on, where's the 'arm? We swim in the same river.

LIZZIE. I don't think that's true.

ANNIE. Course we do. You're a model, I'm a model. What? Just cuz I done tricks and you didn't? That don't make you Queen of England.

LIZZIE. I'm not a model any more, I'm an artist.

ANNIE. Oh, what's the difference? What? It's only a dance round an easel. You step one side, I step the other – well, pardon me if I don't care – it's not real life. What's it for? It 'angs on a wall. It dun't keep you warm. You can't eat it. What is it? Paint stains on a bit of canvas. Smudges on paper. Your smudges are better than 'is – 'is smudges are better than yours. Who cares?

LIZZIE. *I* care! Many people care and *I* care! Or are we all just animals on two legs with nothing in our heads but what to eat and what to burn for a fire? Are all the feelings of our hearts to be ignored? Unremembered? Worthless? Numberless? As animals are numberless? Our lives must have meaning! Or else why live? I'm sorry. I'm so sorry. I didn't mean to be rude.

HUNT *and* ROSSETTI *re-enter.*

HUNT. Annie, we're leaving now.

ANNIE. Oh, don't ask me, will ya, just tell me. I'm a dog: woof, woof.

ROSSETTI. Goodbye, Annie. I'll see you soon.

ANNIE. Yeah. 'Ope so.

HUNT. Annie!

ANNIE. Miss Siddal. Nice to meet another model.

HUNT. Annie!

The sound of a front door knocker.

ROSSETTI. Ruskin.

HUNT. Well, we're going. We're going.

ROSSETTI. Yes, you are.

ROSSETTI *exits to let* RUSKIN *in.*

LIZZIE. Miss Miller... Annie. If you would like to meet on some other / occasion.

ANNIE. No, you're all right. I ain't good with women. I'm better with men.

ROSSETTI *enters with* RUSKIN.

RUSKIN (*to* HUNT). Holman. My dear fellow. What a surprise.

HUNT. John. We're just leaving. Oh. May I present Miss Annie Miller. Mr John Ruskin.

RUSKIN. How do you do.

ANNIE. I do very well, thank you, John, 'ow do you do?

RUSKIN. I... Well, I...

HUNT. We're going, John.

ROSSETTI. They are just going, John.

ANNIE. Yep. We're going, John.

HUNT. So. Goodbye. Goodbye.

ANNIE. Bye.

HUNT *and* ANNIE *leave.*

RUSKIN. Who was that person?

ROSSETTI. Annie?

RUSKIN. She seemed rather earthy.

ROSSETTI. She's a model, John.

RUSKIN. Is Hunt stepping out with a model?

ROSSETTI. I believe he may be.

RUSKIN. Hmm. (*To* LIZZIE.) My dear. We have not been introduced, but I feel sure it is you I've come to see.

ROSSETTI. John, may I present Miss Elizabeth Siddal. Lizzie, this is John Ruskin.

LIZZIE *curtsies*.

LIZZIE. How do you do, sir.

RUSKIN. Miss Siddal. This is a treat. I have gazed upon your features innumerable times in pencil form. This man has not ceased drawing you these three years. I have examined you in outline, tone, line and tone, wet drawing, and in colour. But in all that work there was one feature which I could not discern, thus making an encounter with you a necessity.

LIZZIE. What feature, sir?

RUSKIN. Your voice. I had to hear your voice. Say something, Miss Siddal.

LIZZIE. I... don't know what you'd have me say... However, what I would wish to say to you is how wonderfully you describe the paintings of Turner in *Modern Painters, Volume One*. I have never read a more enthralling description of art.

RUSKIN (*to* ROSSETTI). This is what I came for. This is what I wanted to hear. Miss Siddal, you speak well, you do speak well. Say something else. What can I get you to say?

LIZZIE. Perhaps if we engage in conversation naturally, sir.

ROSSETTI. Will you take tea, John?

RUSKIN. Alas, I cannot. This is where the day has taken a discouraging turn of events. The truth is, I nearly didn't come here at all.

ROSSETTI. Oh dear.

RUSKIN. But then I knew how disappointed you both would be, and so I came but I have dismal news; this present visit can only be fleeting.

LIZZIE. Is there some trouble, Mr Ruskin?

RUSKIN. One of timing. I was in the very act of leaving my house, when a messenger came from Lidgate – my lawyer – sends his compliments and could he trouble me for an urgent interview?

ROSSETTI. Is that because of...? /

RUSKIN. Don't ask.

ROSSETTI. I won't.

RUSKIN. She's made her bed. Now she can lie in it. Are you still in touch with Millais?

ROSSETTI. No. No.

RUSKIN. You Pre-Raphaelites all made such play of your sincerity. And now I wear a cuckold's horns. How is your health, my dear? That business with *Ophelia* – I hope it has not left you with permanent damage?

LIZZIE. No, sir.

ROSSETTI. Her lungs are weaker, John.

RUSKIN. Are they? In that case, you must see my doctor. Acland is very capable; he can treat anything. (*To* ROSSETTI.) Even women's complaints.

ROSSETTI. Really?

RUSKIN. Oh yes.

RUSKIN *smiles. The moment has come.*

Look at you. Graceful and patient. Exactly as I had imagined. Gabriel pressed some work of yours into my hands. Did he tell you that I liked it?

LIZZIE. Yes, Mr Ruskin, he did.

RUSKIN. There are some desperate faults, Miss Siddal. I tell you now the people in your pictures will never walk, for they stand on legs that have no muscle.

ROSSETTI. She couldn't go to life class.

RUSKIN. Of course she couldn't, she's a woman. She could study statues though.

ROSSETTI. Quite. (*To* LIZZIE.) Statues.

RUSKIN (*to* LIZZIE). Do not distress yourself, my dear. I have not come to pick at threads. Your pictures are naive. That is their strength. They speak to the heart. Let me be brief. I wish to own your work.

LIZZIE. Own it?

RUSKIN. All of it. I'd like to buy it. That folder there. How much? How much do you want for it?

ROSSETTI. Twenty... five. Twenty-five pounds.

RUSKIN. I'll give you thirty. Would that be acceptable?

ROSSETTI. Yes. Very. Completely.

RUSKIN. Good.

LIZZIE. You're buying *all* my work?

RUSKIN. Is that agreeable?

LIZZIE. Yes, Mr Ruskin. It is agreeable.

RUSKIN. Excellent! Have I made you happy? I have? You don't know how it cheers a man to see a woman smile. I wanted to meet you. I wanted to be sure. I am sure. Here's what I propose... I'd like to patronise a woman. It would be a treat for me. How would it suit if I were to pay you an allowance of... a hundred and fifty a year?

ROSSETTI. A hundred and fifty?

RUSKIN. What do you think?

ROSSETTI. Pounds?

RUSKIN. Would that be helpful?

ROSSETTI. A year?

LIZZIE. It would be astonishing, sir.

RUSKIN. Well, I have astonished people all my life.

ROSSETTI. A hundred and fifty a year!

LIZZIE. And in return?

RUSKIN. What, my dear?

LIZZIE. What you would require in return?

RUSKIN. Your work.

LIZZIE. All of it?

RUSKIN. Yes.

LIZZIE. Everything?

RUSKIN. Yes.

LIZZIE. You will keep everything?

RUSKIN. Yes. Is that a problem?

LIZZIE. So you would be keeping my work, *and* my person?

    RUSKIN *hesitates*.

ROSSETTI. She accepts. You do. It's done. She does. We accept.

RUSKIN (*to* LIZZIE). Do you accept?

    LIZZIE *hesitates*.

LIZZIE.... Yes. I do. Thank you. I accept.

RUSKIN. Good. Then it is done. How I wish I could stay to share your pleasure. However, I must take arms against a sea of troubles. Next Tuesday. Come to my house, in the afternoon, both of you. We'll have tea.

    RUSKIN *holds out his hand*. LIZZIE *shakes it*.

Miss Siddal. *Au revoir.* I have lots to teach you. Oh. Yes. Don't paint.

LIZZIE. I'm sorry?

RUSKIN. You must not paint. Not till you can draw. Drawing must be studied first. You must draw from nature; simple objects to start: a flower, a rock.

LIZZIE. A rock?

RUSKIN. I myself have made studies of a rock.

LIZZIE. And if I feel no passion for a rock, sir?

RUSKIN. You must.

ROSSETTI. She will. I know she will.

RUSKIN. Of course she will. (*To* LIZZIE.) You will. And I will guide your every mark. You'll never draw unaided again. I have you. Don't worry. What a novelty this will be.

RUSKIN *holds out his hand to* ROSSETTI.

Gabriel.

ROSSETTI. John.

RUSKIN. You owe me a picture. I paid in advance. Where's the picture?

ROSSETTI. I haven't done it.

RUSKIN. Why not?

ROSSETTI. I was too busy spending your money.

RUSKIN. *Au revoir.*

RUSKIN *goes, waving.*

ROSSETTI. *Au revoir…* Lizzie!

LIZZIE. What have I done?

ROSSETTI. You have conquered Ruskin!

LIZZIE. Have I? Is that what I have done?

ROSSETTI. You are splendiferous! You are magnificent! You are rich!

LIZZIE. I am. Yes. I am!… Or have I signed my life away?

ROSSETTI. No, no, no! You are an artist!

LIZZIE. Yes! I am an artist!… who must not paint. I must not / paint.

ROSSETTI. Ignore him.

LIZZIE. I can't ignore / him.

ROSSETTI. Ignore him, fob him off. Take his tin! A hundred and fifty! That's money! That's proper coin! That's what a vicar earns in a year! And you won't even have to go to church on Sundays!

LIZZIE. Yes! And does he own me?

ROSSETTI. No, he doesn't own you; he sustains you.

LIZZIE. I feel as if I have given something away.

ROSSETTI. You haven't. You haven't. You are not giving, you are taking – taking his tin! Why are you not dancing? Why? You are an artist *and* being paid! /

LIZZIE. Yes. /

ROSSETTI. A hundred and fifty!

LIZZIE. So much money! That's nearly… more than I can count – I can give my mother some / money.

ROSSETTI. You can buy me a dinner.

LIZZIE. I can buy you a year of dinners.

ROSSETTI. A hundred and fifty pounds. That's enough to rent your own apartment.

LIZZIE (*a beat*). Yes.

ROSSETTI. You could get your own apartment.

LIZZIE. Yes. I *could* get my own apartment.

ROSSETTI. *Will* you get your own apartment?

LIZZIE.…I *could*.

ROSSETTI. Of course you could. You should.

LIZZIE. Live on my own?

ROSSETTI. Yes. Oh yes. It's the only way to be. Think of it, Liz. Your own apartment.

LIZZIE. Why would I want to live on my own?

ROSSETTI. So you could work.

LIZZIE.…I always thought I'd marry. And work.

ROSSETTI. But now you are independent.

LIZZIE. Am I?

ROSSETTI. How wonderful to be independent. To be free to come and go as you please, completely unencumbered. Believe me, Liz, that's how an artist should live.

LIZZIE. …Gabriel. You know my expectations. We are a pair. You've said yourself, we are the Sun and the Moon. We are balancing opposites, are we not? We are lovers.

ROSSETTI. I agree.

LIZZIE. Then…?

ROSSETTI. I agree. Balance. Is everything. Keeping it. Keeping our lives in balance. Just so. A delicate equilibrium.

LIZZIE. You do intend to marry me?

ROSSETTI. All in good time.

LIZZIE. Wouldn't this then be a moment to… consider…

ROSSETTI. What?

LIZZIE. Asking me?

ROSSETTI. I don't think so. Do you? Why upset the equilibrium now?

LIZZIE. What upset would there be? You wish to marry?

ROSSETTI. Yes.

LIZZIE. You wish to have me for your wife?

ROSSETTI. Yes.

LIZZIE. Then, in God's name, Gabriel, what do you say?

ROSSETTI. …It is not always better to possess. To yearn for something… doesn't that make life more intense? All the great stories are stories of longing: Orpheus, Troilus, Dante. To have the-thing-we-want-most within our reach and yet to have it not. Only in the midst of longing do we know that we're alive.

LIZZIE. I know very well that I am alive, Gabriel! I do not need to play a game to feel that! Why do you speak like a lawyer when you should speak like a poet?

ROSSETTI. I do speak like a poet.

LIZZIE. You speak like a scoundrel!

Blackout.

End of Act One.

ACT TWO

Scene One

A GREENGROCER *stands outside his shop.*

LIZZIE *approaches.*

GREENGROCER. All right, darlin'? What can I do for you?
Plums? Apples? Pears? I tell you what I 'ave got. Got some
nice Ribston Pippins come up from Kent – they come up
yesterday.

LIZZIE. Do you have laudanum?

GREENGROCER. Laudanum? Yes. Ah, well now I say yes,
only we've 'ad a woman up Percy Street 'ad twins six
months ago. She's been buying up the laudanum ever since.
She drinks it – *they* drinks it. 'Ang about. (*Shouts to someone
offstage.*) *Mum!*

MOTHER (*off*). What?

GREENGROCER. We got any laudanum left?

MOTHER (*off*). Is that Mrs Marsh?

GREENGROCER. No.

MOTHER (*off*). 'Ow are the twins?

GREENGROCER. It's not Mrs Marsh.

MOTHER (*off*) Oh. We should 'ave one behind the scabby
Worcesters.

GREENGROCER (*to himself*). Behind the scabby Worcesters.

He looks behind a basket of apples.

(*To* LIZZIE.) They're nice Worcesters actually if you scrape
the scabs off. That's the trouble with people, they want all
their fruit to look pretty. But that's not natural, is it. We can't

all look pretty. Some of us are scabby Worcesters. (*Picks up a bottle of laudanum.*) There we go. Ninepence.

LIZZIE *hands over the money. The* GREENGROCER *gives her the bottle.*

Now. If it's an infant – five drops. If it's an adult – thirty drops. It's on the label, but not everyone can read, can they. Look after yourself.

LIZZIE *walks five paces, stops, uncorks the bottle and drinks.*

She walks into her small apartment. There are no lights yet. An easel, two chairs, a table. She puts the bottle of laudanum on the table next to a glass.

LIZZIE *sits down. The lights go up.* RUSKIN *enters.*

RUSKIN. I do wish for once you wouldn't look so weary when I come here. I am taking infinite pains over your work – I don't believe any man alive could be more diligent in pointing out your errors – and yet I am treated to a miserable countenance. I do think a sullen face, particularly in a woman, is very unappealing. Are you ill?

LIZZIE. No.

RUSKIN. You can't be well.

LIZZIE. Your doctor said I'm not ill.

RUSKIN. That's not true. What Acland said was he could find 'no disease'. However, 'if you were prone to moods and melancholy' – which I told him you *were* – then he thought 'the cause lay in mental power long pent-up'. That is not good, particularly for a woman. He recommended the juice of the poppy. Are you taking it?

LIZZIE. Yes.

RUSKIN. Have you taken some today?

LIZZIE. Yes.

RUSKIN. And yet you are not at ease.

LIZZIE. It's worn off.

RUSKIN. Then why not take some more? You are much happier when you've had some.

LIZZIE. Gabriel's coming later. I'll take some more when he's here.

RUSKIN. You don't want to take some now while I'm here?

LIZZIE. No I don't.

RUSKIN. I get more cordiality from a spaniel. This is the life you wanted, isn't it? Your own little apartment. Your own paints. No other woman that I know of can boast as much.

LIZZIE. I had not thought to feel so lonely.

RUSKIN. You know, whenever I'm unhappy, I draw pictures. Art compensates us for life. In art, we can all come face to face with the ideal.

LIZZIE. Instead of living it? Why? Why draw it? Why not live it?

RUSKIN. We can't always live it. Art is a way of touching it.

LIZZIE. And still not having it. No compensation then.

RUSKIN. Oh very well, very well, very well. I cannot remain silent any longer. I have watched you these two years and seen it growing worse and worse. I cannot stand by and let two people ruin their lives.

LIZZIE. Of what subject do you speak, sir?

RUSKIN. Everybody knows that you and Gabriel should be married.

LIZZIE. Oh, Mr Ruskin, please / don't.

RUSKIN. Yes. I / must.

LIZZIE. I beg you, sir, no, please, don't / speak of it.

RUSKIN. I cannot remain / silent.

LIZZIE. Can you not see how humiliating it would be to have to discuss such a private matter / with you?

RUSKIN. I cannot help / it.

LIZZIE. I do not wish to discuss / it.

RUSKIN. I must / speak.

LIZZIE. I do not wish to discuss a matter of feeling with *you*!

Pause.

RUSKIN. You are nearly thirty – still not married – it was
    perfectly obvious to me what needed to be done, which is
    why I did what I did.

LIZZIE. What? What did you do?

RUSKIN. I take it, if Gabriel were to ask you, you would say
    yes?

LIZZIE. He has not asked me.

RUSKIN. You would be willing though?

LIZZIE. He has not asked me.

RUSKIN. Oh, my dear girl, if he asked you, what would you
    say?

LIZZIE. He has not asked!

RUSKIN. He will ask… He will ask this afternoon. That is
    what I have managed to bring about. You think me just a
    meddlesome man, but I am, I hope, capable still of stooping
    from my saddle when I see a damsel in distress.

LIZZIE. What do you mean?

RUSKIN. I am not the ogre you paint me. I am trying to do you
    a kindness.

LIZZIE. What do you mean, 'he will ask this afternoon'?

RUSKIN. I have had a conversation with Gabriel. A proper
    conversation. Why – I asked him – why the delay? Everybody
    knows you two should marry. Everybody's known for years
    you should marry. Why has he not asked you?

LIZZIE. And he said? What did he say?

RUSKIN. He said he meant to. He always meant to. At first, he
    couldn't ask, he had no money to sustain a marriage. Then,

when he had money, there was an incident. You offended his mother.

LIZZIE. No I didn't.

RUSKIN. When you met her.

LIZZIE. I didn't offend her. When I met her – at long last – she asked me if my father was in trade. I said he was. And then a frost fell in the room. My offence was my parentage.

RUSKIN. Well, whatever it was. In any event, Time dragged on. Time plays its part, doesn't it. Time is the enemy, especially of we romantics. And Time has led us to this pass, where poor Gabriel was wondering if perhaps it is too late after all?

LIZZIE. Too late?

RUSKIN. Now that you're ill.

LIZZIE. I'm not ill.

RUSKIN. You say you're not ill.

LIZZIE. I am not ill, I am not ill. Because a woman doesn't smile, it doesn't mean she's ill. It means she has feelings. And feelings need to be attended to.

RUSKIN. Well then. Bizarrely, I may be the man to pay them attention. To conclude, I discovered that Gabriel was on the cusp of asking you this month.

LIZZIE. This month?

RUSKIN. This very month, yes. He told me.

LIZZIE. But he didn't. He didn't.

RUSKIN. No.

LIZZIE. Then what in Heaven's name stopped him?

RUSKIN. He didn't think you wanted to.

LIZZIE. He didn't think *I* – ? Why would he think that? Why? Why?

RUSKIN. I don't know. Please remain calm, I am trying to do you a service.

LIZZIE. Yes. Yes, I believe you are. Oh, Mr Ruskin, I have misjudged you. He wants to marry me? He told you?

RUSKIN. I pressed him on that very point. You know Gabriel – skips about like Puck – but I pinned him down. He told me – he said – you are the only woman he ever thought of marrying. He agrees with me, it ought to be done. So, I lent him the money.

LIZZIE.... What money?

RUSKIN. Well, he said he didn't have money for a wedding right now; he'd just bought a pair of peacocks.

LIZZIE. Peacocks?

RUSKIN. Beautiful things but completely useless.

LIZZIE. Yes. That's what he loves. Beautiful things that are completely useless.

RUSKIN. Well, anyway. He has the money now thanks to me. He's coming here. I've done what had to be done.

LIZZIE (*a beat*). I don't know what to say. Mr Ruskin, I am so indebted to you.

RUSKIN. I did what was right. It *is* right. Anyone can see you two are a pair.

LIZZIE. But I misread your concern.

RUSKIN. Yes, you mistook intercession for interference. Now perhaps you might smile?

LIZZIE. Yes.

RUSKIN. And be a little nicer to your benefactor?

LIZZIE. Yes. Yes. Why did he delay so long?

RUSKIN. Gabriel is a butterfly. He likes to flit. He was put upon this earth to infuriate. Never mind, he will ask you today and you'd better say yes.

LIZZIE. Yes. I will. Thank you. Thank you.

RUSKIN. Well. There it is. Now you're happy. Shall we turn to your work? Shall we discuss the mistakes I have found in your last picture?

LIZZIE. No, Mr Ruskin – dear Mr Ruskin – I would not take in a word.

RUSKIN. No. Perhaps you wouldn't. Once again Minerva is rudely brushed aside by Venus. That might be the sound of Love arriving now. I have said nothing. Let him surprise you.

LIZZIE. Mr Ruskin, thank you!

She kisses his cheek.

RUSKIN. Oh. Well. Very fine.

ROSSETTI (*off*). Hello? Hello?

ROSSETTI enters.

RUSKIN. Gabriel, hello. I was just leaving. Lizzie has declined to listen to my comments on her work, as usual. I doubt whether she'll listen to you about anything either.

RUSKIN winks at him, then turns to LIZZIE.

Next time, Herne Hill. I can't come here again. People will gossip. *Au revoir.*

ROSSETTI. Goodbye, John.

LIZZIE. Goodbye, Mr Ruskin. Thank you.

ROSSETTI. Was he unbearable?

LIZZIE. No. No, he wasn't. He was surprisingly thrilling to listen to.

ROSSETTI. Was he? Oh. And how are you?

LIZZIE. I am well. And you? How are you?

ROSSETTI. I'm sorry I haven't visited. I have had such distractions.

LIZZIE. Have you?

ROSSETTI. You wouldn't believe.

LIZZIE. Really?

ROSSETTI. Enormous events are afoot. I am become a juggler. All manner of objects in the air. Did I tell you Ruth Herbert has agreed to sit for me?

LIZZIE. No. Ruth Herbert. How astonishing!

ROSSETTI. Isn't it? She is stunning – stunning! What abundance of beauty. Golden hair.

LIZZIE. Is she your Mary Magdalene?

ROSSETTI. She is. Every morning at half past eleven. She can't come earlier – she doesn't get off stage till late at night – but then I'm busy with something else, too. I haven't told you yet. Something amazing. Can you guess what it is?

LIZZIE *sits, expectantly.*

LIZZIE. No.

ROSSETTI. Guess.

LIZZIE. I can't. Tell me.

ROSSETTI. Helen of Troy.

LIZZIE. ...Helen of Troy?

ROSSETTI. I'm only sketching for now, not painting. But it will be such a painting. It will be the face that launched a thousand ships and left a city rubble.

LIZZIE. Who is sitting for you?

ROSSETTI. Annie Miller.

LIZZIE. Annie Miller.

ROSSETTI. It's early days. I'm squeezing her in when I can. I'm still finishing off Fanny Cornforth. She comes in the afternoon. You remember – the oil? *Bocca Bocciata.*

LIZZIE. 'The kissed mouth.'

ROSSETTI. 'The kissed mouth.' Anyway, I'm exhausted. And this evening I have to go on from here. I have to meet a sponsor – no one you know.

LIZZIE. You're not staying?

ROSSETTI. I can stay for an hour. Do you want to send out for some food? We could eat together before I go.

LIZZIE. You're not staying longer?

ROSSETTI. I can't.

LIZZIE. Can't you?

ROSSETTI. Sorry.

Pause.

Oh. Did you tell Ruskin you put that watercolour in Brown's exhibition? You know if it sells, the money rightly belongs to Ruskin, don't you?

LIZZIE. Ruskin told me you and he met last week.

ROSSETTI. Yes, we did. Don't worry, I didn't mention the painting.

LIZZIE. Ruskin said that you talked about marriage.

ROSSETT....Marriage?

LIZZIE. Yes.

ROSSETTI. No.

LIZZIE. Ruskin said you had.

ROSSETTI. Did he?

LIZZIE. He said you were thinking of proposing – marriage – to me. You didn't have the money. He lent you some.

ROSSETTI. He said that?

LIZZIE. Yes.

ROSSETTI. How extraordinary.

LIZZIE. What is?

ROSSETTI. That he should link the two. It's true he lent me money. I found myself temporarily in want. He mentioned marriage?

LIZZIE. Yes. He said you were coming here today to propose.

ROSSETTI. Well, that's – For a start, he'd no business to say that, even if it were true. And it's not – of course it's not. I mean, it was quite a rum conversation actually. I remember, yes, yes he did ask why we never married. So I explained.

LIZZIE. Did you?

ROSSETTI. Yes.

LIZZIE. What did you say?

ROSSETTI. I explained. How a fire that burns brightly can often die down. Become less fierce. Still warm, but no longer a fire. Like embers… We are still, I hope, firm friends.

Pause.

Are you all right?

LIZZIE. Mm.

ROSSETTI. Do you want your medicine?

LIZZIE. In a minute.

ROSSETTI. To lift your spirits?

LIZZIE. In a minute.

ROSSETTI. It'll make you happier.

LIZZIE. In a minute!

Pause.

I am used goods. Who would have me now? I shall be thirty soon. No longer a maid and never a wife. You said I was your true love.

ROSSETTI. You were.

Pause.

LIZZIE *rises and goes to the laudanum bottle on the table.*

LIZZIE. When did I become this thing? How is it I passed from a love into a duty?

ROSSETTI. Is this how you want to spend the hour?

LIZZIE. What?

ROSSETTI. Going over old ground?

LIZZIE. 'Old ground'?

She uncorks the bottle and starts to let liquid fall into the glass.

ROSSETTI. Digging up the past. Would not this be better left for another occasion? When you are more yourself?

LIZZIE. I am myself now.

She drinks.

ROSSETTI. You are taking medicine.

LIZZIE. I hate it! I hate taking it! I take it to dull the pain in my heart. I want to be loved. Is that an illness? How convenient for you! To have me ill! No woman who was ill was ever bride. Why would you want me to be healthy?

ROSSETTI. That is a dreadful slander.

LIZZIE. And yet it's true.

ROSSETTI. I do not wish you ill.

LIZZIE. And yet if I were healthy...?

ROSSETTI. What? What? What do you want me to say?

LIZZIE. The very thing you cannot! God help me!

Pause.

Someone bought my painting.

ROSSETTI. What?

LIZZIE. Brown's exhibition. My painting sold on merit.

ROSSETTI. That's wonderful news.

LIZZIE. Yes. Wonderful.

ROSSETTI. You look so sour.

LIZZIE. Well then, how lucky that we did not make it into church. What a sorry bargain I would have made at the altar. A woman you no longer love, who slanders you and looks so sour... I wrote you a poem. Would you like to hear it?

ROSSETTI....If you like.

LIZZIE. Would you like to hear it?

ROSSETTI. Yes.

LIZZIE. You really wish to hear it?

ROSSETTI. Yes. Read it to me.

LIZZIE. I don't need to read it! It is carved on my heart!

Pause.

Sit down then.

ROSSETTI *sits and waits for* LIZZIE *to begin.*

> 'Ope not thy lips, thou foolish one,
> Nor turn to me thy face;
> The blasts of Heaven shall strike thee down
> Ere I will give thee grace.
>
> Take thou thy shadow from my path,
> Nor turn to me and pray;
> The wild wild winds thy dirge may sing
> Ere I will bid thee stay.
>
> Turn thou away thy false dark eyes,
> Nor gaze upon my face;
> Great love I bore thee: now great hate
> Sits grimly in its place.
>
> All changes pass me like a dream,
> I neither sing nor pray;
> And thou art like the poisonous tree
> That stole my life away.'

Pause.

Do you like it? Do you like my poem? It is, I think, sincere.

Pause.

I shall write to Mr Ruskin and tell him I no longer require his allowance.

ROSSETTI (*a beat*). Why would you do that?

LIZZIE. I am an artist now, like you.

ROSSETTI. It's one painting.

LIZZIE. *You* have sold, *I* have sold. I am your equal. I shall make my own way in the world.

ROSSETTI. But... it is one small watercolour.

LIZZIE. Then I will do other small watercolours, I will flood the world with watercolours, I will *bleed* watercolours!

ROSSETTI. Then do so, do so. But it does not make sense to cast off Ruskin's money. Why? Why do that?

LIZZIE. Because it's *over*, Gabriel! All *over*! I renounce *him*! I renounce his *money*! I renounce *you*!

Scene Two

Dusk. Sheffield School of Art. The Principal's Office.

The Principal is a Yorkshireman, MR MITCHELL. *He is searching for something amidst the papers on his desk.*

MITCHELL (*to an offstage secretary*). Are you still there, Mrs Fimber? Do you have that speech for the South Yorkshire Steelmakers' Guild? Hello? Oh. No. It's all right, Mrs Fimber, I've found it – on my desk. (*To himself.*) So there's no bloody escape. Thirty self-satisfied Yorkshire businessmen, full of roast lamb and liquor. And I get up and I say, 'Mr Chairman, Members of the Guild, it is an honour to speak to you tonight. My name is Mitchell, I am Principal of Sheffield College of Art, and I am here to ask for donations'... They'll hear the laughter in Wakefield. It'll be like a sudden gust of brandy breath. 'I know what you're thinking, gentlemen. Donations? This is Yorkshire. You don't get owt for nowt round here. What am I offering *you*? What can I offer men like you – you makers, you doers, you great men of Sheffield? For you are great. There are giants in this very room. Somewhere in this room, the inventor of the Norfolk knife; somewhere else, the creator of the lobster-spring penknife; and also, I am told, a

man who this year transformed the process of galvanising
steel. I could go on – for this room is awash with greatness –
and I am proud. There is no city in Europe can outdo
Sheffield for champions of manufacture. I ask only one
question. When your day's work is done, the food eaten, the
table cleared and you and your loved ones sit round the fire,
what do you see? Do you see beauty? Do you see love? What
vistas lift the spirit? What images inspire your children? The
pictures that surround us alter how we feel inside. Where do
these images come from? I will tell you where they come
from: artists.'

MITCHELL *stops and calls out.*

Is that you, Mrs Fimber? Are you still there?

LIZZIE *enters. She is edgy and distracted.*

LIZZIE. Mr Mitchell, dear Mr Mitchell, hello, how are you, are
you well? I couldn't see your secretary. Is it all right if I come
in? I am in, but I could go out again. Should I go out / again?

MITCHELL. No, no, please, come in, Miss Siddal.

LIZZIE. Has Mrs Fimber gone home?

MITCHELL. I expect she has.

LIZZIE. Is she ill?

MITCHELL. No. Her day finishes at six.

LIZZIE. Oh dear. Does that mean I'm – I am, aren't I – I'm late.

MITCHELL. It was yesterday, Miss Siddal. Our appointment.

LIZZIE. Yesterday?

MITCHELL. Not to worry. We can do it now. Won't you sit
down?

LIZZIE *sits. So does* MITCHELL.

How are you feeling?

LIZZIE. I am well, thank you.

MITCHELL. I am glad to hear it.

LIZZIE. Will we be long, do you think? My cousin's waiting for me downstairs.

MITCHELL. Not long, no. I'll get straight to the point, why not? Mr Allison came to see me. He tells me you're leaving Sheffield. I wondered why that could be.

LIZZIE *gets up*.

LIZZIE. Do you mind if I don't sit, Mr Mitchell? I get so cold. I'd rather...

MITCHELL. As you wish.

LIZZIE. Thank you. Mm. I'm sorry. What was your question?

MITCHELL. I wondered if you might tell me your reason for going.

LIZZIE. Oh. Yes. It's private.

MITCHELL. I understand. Of course.

LIZZIE. So. If that's all you wanted...

MITCHELL. I do have a duty to ask though. Is there some problem in the College? Your tutor – some find Mr Allison a bit too direct.

LIZZIE. No. I like the way he speaks.

MITCHELL. Do you? Good. Good. And mockery. I hear there was mockery from other students. They find your clothes eccentric or some such nonsense. Does that trouble you?

LIZZIE. No. They are younger than me. The young need someone to ridicule.

MITCHELL. Is it your health? How is your health? You missed lessons.

LIZZIE. It's better. My health is better. It is. I am taking more medicine.

MITCHELL. I don't mean to / pry, Miss Siddal.

LIZZIE. I have no money, Mr Mitchell. I've run out. My cousin has been very kind, but now she needs to rent out my room. I

am going back to London. My mother knows a dress shop
needs a seamstress. That's why I'm leaving.

MITCHELL *gets up*.

MITCHELL. Well then. That's settled. I won't let you go.

LIZZIE. I beg your / pardon?

MITCHELL. I won't let you go. And here's the reason. Can you
name me ten women artists? Five? Three? Why are there no
women artists? Why? Women are dextrous; they have eyes;
they have feelings. They make marvellous tapestries. Why
not marvellous paintings?

LIZZIE. I'm sorry, Mr Mitchell, are you asking me?

MITCHELL. You're a woman, Miss Siddal. You've no say in
the art world. None. Who can represent you?

LIZZIE. No one.

MITCHELL. I will.

LIZZIE.... You?

MITCHELL. I will. Miss Siddal, your story – what you've done
– no one has ever done. For a model to climb down from the
gallery wall and pick up the paintbrushes herself. Whoever
heard of that before? A woman. How many women painters
are there? – one or two who dabble in drawing rooms –
they've money and leisure. But you... had nothing. To start
with nothing, and to *do* work, *show* work, *sell* work. From
scratch to make yourself an artist – a woman artist. To come
up here and insist on learning to draw better... You're too
important to be allowed to fade into nothingness.

This is all a revelation to LIZZIE.

LIZZIE. Do you really think that?

MITCHELL. Yes. I do. Now listen carefully. There are men
round here made pots of money: iron-makers, steel-makers,
gun-makers, silver-platers. They live in those big houses up
at High Hazels. How would it be if I acted for you? If I
showed them your work?

LIZZIE. Would they like my painting?

MITCHELL. Some would, some wouldn't. But you'd sell enough to keep going. If a woman artist could keep going, wouldn't that be wonderful?

LIZZIE. Oh, Mr Mitchell.

MITCHELL. What do you say?

LIZZIE. I had a dream of doing this.

MITCHELL. Well then? What do you say?

LIZZIE.…I am so sorry to have to turn you down.

A beat.

MITCHELL. I beg pardon?

LIZZIE. To turn your offer down. So sorry.

MITCHELL. You're turning me down?

LIZZIE. I've had enough, Mr Mitchell. I've, I've had enough. Of art, and artists. I detest artists. Why would I want to be one?

MITCHELL. You detest / artists?

LIZZIE. Their business is deceit.

MITCHELL. No, no, that's nonsense – that's… Why would you say / that?

LIZZIE. I do not wish to argue with you, sir. /

MITCHELL. Artists – artists are the seekers after truth.

LIZZIE. How little you know. How little. It's illusion. It's paint. They trick the eyes – so then the eyes can dupe the heart. There's no truth in it, it's pigment. You can't believe in pigment. A false heart can paint true love. It doesn't make the painter virtuous. Where's the virtue? Only in the brushwork.

A beat.

MITCHELL. My dear woman.

LIZZIE. I'd like to leave now, please, if you don't mind.

MITCHELL. There's no need to go / quite so…

LIZZIE. Yes, now, if you don't mind, / sir.

MITCHELL. We should talk about this surely. /

LIZZIE. I don't wish to / talk, Mr Mitchell.

MITCHELL. Just for a / minute.

LIZZIE. I do not wish to stay, sir, please! I wish to leave!

Pause.

MITCHELL. I didn't mean to upset you.

LIZZIE. It's because you are kind.

She starts to go.

MITCHELL. Oh. Miss Siddal. I should have said – I've had a letter, from Mr Ruskin.

LIZZIE *stops.*

John Ruskin. He didn't have your address. He wrote to me.

LIZZIE *continues to exit.*

He sends his compliments. He hopes to arrange a meeting with you and Mr Rossetti.

LIZZIE *stops.* MITCHELL *has the letter in his hand.* LIZZIE *hesitates, then takes it.*

Scene Three

An apartment overlooking Blackfriars Bridge. A couple of chairs and a table. On the table is a bottle of laudanum and a glass.

ROSSETTI *and* HUNT.

HUNT. I regret it being such a long time.

ROSSETTI. Me too.

HUNT. And now you're going to think I'm here because I want something.

ROSSETTI. No, of course not.

HUNT. I do want something.

ROSSETTI. Do you?

HUNT. Annie Miller is sitting for you.

ROSSETTI. She is.

HUNT. I wondered if I could see her?

ROSSETTI. Annie?

HUNT. Yes.

ROSSETTI. She didn't come today.

HUNT. Didn't she?

ROSSETTI. No.

HUNT. Will she be coming tomorrow?

ROSSETTI. Possibly… Would you like me to give her a message? If I see her?

HUNT. Would you tell her she's a slut and a whore? And I'll see her rot in Hell before I pay her any more money? And the letters which she says she has – aye, there's the irony – I paid for her reading lessons – those letters, which she claims contain promises of marriage – well, tell her, no more money. None. Unless she hand over the letters. In which case, I will give her one more five-pound note and two sovereigns for luck. Could you remember that?

ROSSETTI. I think so.

HUNT. Thank you. How is Lizzie?

ROSSETTI. Not well.

HUNT. You didn't invite me to the wedding.

ROSSETTI. I didn't invite anyone to the wedding.

HUNT. The rumour I heard – after Sheffield – she was quite ill.

ROSSETTI. She was. Ruskin said I should go and see her. She was in an awful state, couldn't eat, taking a deal of laudanum, but not much else. Some days, hardly conscious.

HUNT. Can't have been the courtship you always dreamed of.

ROSSETTI. Everyone thought she was dying. I felt such pity. So I proposed.

HUNT. You proposed because you thought she was dying?

ROSSETTI. Yes.

HUNT. But she didn't die.

ROSSETTI. No.

Pause.

HUNT. Well, well done. You rescued a damsel in distress.

ROSSETTI. I did, didn't I. In fact, the first year of our marriage, she rallied. We were almost like a proper – I don't know if you heard – We – She was delivered of a dead child.

HUNT. Oh, my dear chap.

ROSSETTI. A daughter... I would have had a daughter.

HUNT. How things turn out. Me tangled up with a whore, and you... Not the romance you'd have written for your own life, is it. (*New subject.*) What are you painting? More women's heads? You do like women's heads, if you don't mind my saying. As if you've only just discovered them. *Fair Rosamund* – I mean, it's just a woman's head. You can give it the title *Fair Rosamund* and pop in a silk thread but when all is said / and done –

ROSSETTI. Maniac.

HUNT. Am I being insulting?

ROSSETTI. Yes.

HUNT. Perhaps I should be off.

He rises.

You know what I think? It was wrong to encourage her. As an artist, I mean. Women, for some reason, don't have the tenacity.

ROSSETTI. Lizzie's work is not negligible.

HUNT. It's not extraordinary though. If it were extraordinary, you could forgive her being ill all the time.

ROSSETTI. Is there anything else you wanted?

HUNT. Should I see Lizzie? Before I go?

ROSSETTI. She's not good for company.

HUNT....Next time. You'll give Annie my message?

ROSSETTI. Absolutely. 'Slut, whore, rot in Hell, letters, nothing, unless, five-pound note and two sovereigns.' Is that it?

HUNT. More or less.

They shake hands.

My dear chap.

ROSSETTI. Goodbye.

HUNT *goes.*

ROSSETTI *waits, then speaks.*

I'd wait five minutes, in case he's loitering outside.

ANNIE *appears.*

ANNIE. I know what he wrote well enough. I've 'ad a lawyer read 'em over. Breach of promise. I'll see him in court.

ROSSETTI. Take the money, Annie.

ANNIE. Five and two sovereigns?

ROSSETTI. Marry Captain Thompson.

ANNIE. I might. I might marry the Captain.

ROSSETTI. A fiver and two sovereigns would buy a wedding dress.

ANNIE. If I marry the Captain, he'll pay for the dress. If I take the five and two, that'll be mine.

ROSSETTI. I need to tidy up. See you tomorrow.

ANNIE. Yeah. See you tomorrow.

ROSSETTI *exits towards his studio.*

ANNIE *walks over to the table. Picks up the laudanum bottle. Uncorks it. Sniffs.*

LIZZIE *appears. She is carrying what looks like a baby wrapped in a blanket; except that the blankets are wrapped around nothing.*

ANNIE. I'm not stoppin'.

LIZZIE. Where's Gabriel?

ANNIE. 'E won't be long. My aunt swallowed a bottle of this – never woke up. She was Rother'ithe really but they buried 'er in Stepney. Rother'ithe was sniffy 'bout the coroner's report. They don't care in Stepney.

LIZZIE. You're that whore.

ANNIE. Oh, don't take on. We're not doin' nothin' no more. Poor bloke's as sad as you are. Bless ya. You'll be all right, you can have another. You got the ring on, that's the main thing. You ain't working in no 'at shop now. And I ain't on the game. We done all right.

LIZZIE. I'm sorry if I haven't been your friend.

ANNIE. Tch. Look at ya. You eatin'? You need to eat.

LIZZIE. I can't eat, I vomit. Will you stay with me?

ANNIE. I can't do that, dearie.

LIZZIE. I'll let you see my daughter. Would you like to? Look.

LIZZIE *reaches into the blankets and takes out a paper drawing.*

Gabriel drew her. Such a delicate face.

ANNIE *takes the drawing and looks.*

He wrote a poem underneath. You can read it if you like.

ANNIE. I don't read too good.

LIZZIE. Please.

ANNIE. I can't. I never got the 'ang of it. Didn't see the point.

LIZZIE (*doesn't read, she knows it by heart.*)
    '...This is her picture as she was:
    It seems a thing to wonder on,
    As though mine image in the glass
    Should tarry when myself am gone.
    I gaze until she seems to stir,
    And yet the earth is over her.'

ANNIE. Nice. Yeah. It rhymes. Must be a comfort.

ROSSETTI *re-enters.* ANNIE *sees him.*

Gabriel's come now.

LIZZIE. Thank you so much for visiting. Please come again.

ANNIE. Course.

ANNIE *looks at* ROSSETTI *and leaves.*

LIZZIE (*to the bundle*). Gabriel's here. Gabriel's here.

ROSSETTI. I have to go out soon.

LIZZIE. No.

ROSSETTI. Yes. I have to. You'll be all right, if I go out?

LIZZIE. You won't leave me though.

ROSSETTI. Yes. I just said, I will have to go out.

LIZZIE. Why?

ROSSETTI. I am teaching.

LIZZIE (*a beat*). Why?

ROSSETTI. It's Monday. I teach art. For Ruskin. At the Working Men's Club.

LIZZIE. You're going out to teach art?

ROSSETTI. Yes.

LIZZIE. I feel cold, Gabriel. I'm cold. I'm always cold when you're not here.

ROSSETTI. I'm here now and yet you are cold now.

LIZZIE. Yes! (*Then, seeing and accepting the logic.*) Oh. Yes.

ROSSETTI (*making a move*). So.

LIZZIE. The clothes.

ROSSETTI. What?

LIZZIE. For the baby.

ROSSETTI. What about them?

LIZZIE. We must keep them.

ROSSETTI. You said I should give them away.

LIZZIE. No, we must keep them.

ROSSETTI. Why?

LIZZIE. For another baby.

ROSSETTI. There won't be another baby.

LIZZIE. We might have another.

ROSSETTI. We won't.

LIZZIE. We might.

ROSSETTI. We won't.

LIZZIE. We might. /

ROSSETTI. You are sick. There's no question of another child.

LIZZIE. Yes. I don't mean now. Not now. In the future.

   Pause.

ROSSETTI. So.

LIZZIE. Gabriel, I think I'm going to die tonight.

ROSSETTI. No. /

LIZZIE. I think so. /

ROSSETTI. No. You're not. You're fine.

LIZZIE. I'm not.

ROSSETTI. You're / fine.

LIZZIE. I killed our baby.

ROSSETTI. No.

LIZZIE. That's what you think.

ROSSETTI. I don't.

LIZZIE. My sick body made a sick baby.

ROSSETTI. No.

LIZZIE. That's what Dr Hutchinson said.

ROSSETTI. No he didn't.

LIZZIE. When the mother's sick, the baby dies – he said that.

ROSSETTI. He didn't say that.

LIZZIE. He said it to me.

ROSSETTI. He didn't.

LIZZIE. He wanted to say it. It was in his face. I saw the look.
It's what he thought.

ROSSETTI. He didn't.

LIZZIE. Then why did she die?

ROSSETTI. Nobody knows.

LIZZIE. Was it God's will?

ROSSETTI. No.

LIZZIE. I think it was.

ROSSETTI. No.

LIZZIE. I think it was. I think He killed her.

ROSSETTI. He didn't kill her.

LIZZIE. I think He did, I think He / did.

ROSSETTI. God did not / kill her.

LIZZIE. I think / He did.

ROSSETTI. God did not / kill her!

LIZZIE. Well, somebody killed her, Gabriel! It was either God or me and it wasn't me!… But it must have been me. It must have been me because God is love. So it must have been / me.

ROSSETTI. Stop saying that.

LIZZIE. I would stop, I would, I would if I could, but I can't!

ROSSETTI *strides to the table and pours laudanum into a glass.*

It's what's inside me! And I'm sick inside! I'm sick and I have no life! My life is shrunk to a room and I can't escape and *you* won't help me and *God* won't help me and no one will *help* me! *help* me! / *help* me!

ROSSETTI. Drink this! Drink, drink it, drink! Drink it!

LIZZIE *takes the glass with one hand and drinks. She hands back the glass, then grabs hold of* ROSSETTI*'s coat.*

LIZZIE.…Would you like… to paint me now?

ROSSETTI.…No.

LIZZIE. Why not? I'm the kind of woman you love to paint. I am cursed.

ROSSETTI. I have to go.

ROSSETTI *frees himself from her grasp.*

LIZZIE. No! No! Gabriel, I can't – I can't breathe, I can't breathe, Gabriel!… I can't / breathe!

ROSSETTI. Then sit still! Sit still, for God's sake! Sit! Sit! Sit still!

Pause. LIZZIE *sits as still as she can.*

I'm not a cruel man, Liz. It is simply better if you sit quietly.

LIZZIE. Yes.

ROSSETTI. You used to sit so quietly.

LIZZIE. Yes.

ROSSETTI. Could you do that now?

LIZZIE. Yes.

ROSSETTI. Don't move.

LIZZIE. No.

ROSSETTI. Would you like me to draw you?

LIZZIE. Yes.

ROSSETTI. You'd stay still then?

LIZZIE. Yes.

ROSSETTI. Very well. Close your eyes. I'll begin.

LIZZIE *closes her eyes.*

That's it. Very good.

LIZZIE. I won't / move.

ROSSETTI. Ssssh. Keep quiet for me. And keep very still… That's it… Keep still.

Pause. Then, gradually, silently, ROSSETTI *leaves.*

LIZZIE *is alone but doesn't know it.*

LIZZIE. I am so sorry. To be a burden to you. But I will cure myself, you'll see. We could still have a child. We might – you never know. And I am so grateful, Gabriel. For everything you've done. So grateful. My life was nothing once. Look at me now.

She opens her eyes. She turns her head and sees there is no one there.

…Oh.

She gets up and moves to the table and pours all of the laudanum into the glass. She picks up the picture of her dead daughter, looks at it, and tears it into pieces.

Smudges on paper. Worthless.

She lifts the glass and swallows all of the laudanum.

I think I've had enough.

She walks slowly off.

Instantly, there is the sound of someone banging on a front door with a door knocker.

Scene Four

Night. A house in Chelsea. The knocking continues.

HOWELL (*off*). Gabriel? It's me, Charlie Howell. I'm dying out here. I'm not joking. In fact, I may already be dead. This may be my ghost talking…

ROSSETTI *enters, seven years older, dark circles under his eyes. He carries a candle, walks across the room, places the candle down.*

Gabriel? Can you open the door, please, it's cold, I mean, really freezing, I've just lost a testicle. It froze and dropped off. Look, there it goes now rolling down the street.

ROSSETTI *exits towards the noise.*

It's Charles Howell, Gabriel – your agent. I want to talk to you, for pity's sake.

Offstage, a door opens.

My dear chap, thank God. I can't shake hands just now, my fingers would break.

I could be the first man to die of frostbite in Chelsea.

HOWELL *walks in, followed by* ROSSETTI.

It's very dark in here. Where's your housekeeper?

ROSSETTI. I gave her the night off.

HOWELL. Where's the fire? Aren't you cold?

ROSSETTI. I am cold, yes.

HOWELL. Shall I light a fire?

ROSSETTI. No. I want to feel cold.

HOWELL. What's wrong? What? Something is. You've been shut up in here for a month. What's different? I don't smell any paint. Are you not painting?

ROSSETTI. No.

HOWELL. Why not?

ROSSETTI. It's too cold.

HOWELL.…(*the penny drops*). Oh Lord. It's the tenth. Tonight is the tenth.

ROSSETTI. Yes.

HOWELL. My dear chap.

ROSSETTI. Yes.

HOWELL. How could I not remember? Heavens, you must feel so – How can one put it in words?…

ROSSETTI.

'Then black despair,
The shadow of a starless night, was thrown
Over the world in which I moved alone.'

HOWELL. I say, that's terrific. Did you write that?

ROSSETTI. No. Shelley.

HOWELL. Oh, of course, Shelley – wonderful poet. You poor fellow, how long is it – six? – seven years ago tonight she passed away. You must feel such grief. Well, never you mind what I came for – I shan't even say.

ROSSETTI. Say what?

HOWELL. I shan't say, not now… Although if you really want to know. I suppose you do want to know. Well, if you must know, I came to talk poetry.

ROSSETTI. Poetry?

HOWELL. Yes.

ROSSETTI. I have no poetry.

HOWELL. No.

ROSSETTI. I buried most of my poems in her coffin.

HOWELL. You did. Yes. Your only copy, handwritten – extraordinary thing to do.

ROSSETTI. And now I can't remember them.

HOWELL. No. Might as well not have written them. Anyway, who cares about poems? You poor, poor man. What agonies you must be suffering. I won't even tell you my gossip.

ROSSETTI. Don't. I hate gossip.

HOWELL. So do I. I won't mention Coventry Patmore.

ROSSETTI. Patmore? What about him?

HOWELL. Bell have signed Patmore to bring out a new volume of verse.

ROSSETTI. Patmore?

HOWELL. Yes.

ROSSETTI. He writes twaddle.

HOWELL. Yes. Good twaddle though; sells well…

> 'And she assumed the maiden coy,
> And I adored remorseless charms,
> And then we clapp'd our hands for joy,
> And ran into each other's arms.'

ROSSETTI. For the love of Christ!

HOWELL. Sorry... Anyway, you're right – Patmore – not
exactly Shelley. Now *there's* a writer – Shelley. *His* book
will live for ever. And was it really seven years ago you took
your book of poems – your only copy – and placed it in
Lizzie's coffin? Some would question the sense of that.

ROSSETTI. Let them. I wanted to show her how much I
loved her.

HOWELL. Yes. Although. She was already dead.

ROSSETTI. She killed herself.

HOWELL. The coroner said 'accidental death'. Unless you
know something.

Pause.

Were there any love poems? In the book? The book you put
in her coffin? Any love poems?

ROSSETTI. I can't remember.

HOWELL. Only, love poems are very popular just now... It is a
shame to have a talent like yours write poems that will never
be read. Patmore is read. Rossetti is not. It seems to me a
terrible tragedy that Lizzie, who loved poetry, should be the
very cause now of concealing it.

ROSSETTI. Well. That is how it is.

HOWELL. Not quite... I've made enquiries. It turns out the
book could be recovered.

ROSSETTI. What?

HOWELL. People sometimes bury things, then change their
minds, and want them back.

ROSSETTI. D'you mean... dig her up?

HOWELL. The word they use is 'un-coffined'. I know it sounds
ghastly, but apparently it's perfectly / normal.

ROSSETTI. No!... Good God!

Pause.

HOWELL. No one would ever know.

ROSSETTI. I would know.

HOWELL. Yes. You would know and I would know, but no one else… Well, a chaplain would have to be present… And a lawyer… And the gravediggers… And the Secretary for the Home Office would need to sign the papers; though I am persuaded that's a formality for an artist of your prominence. And there's a man I know can disinfect the book. Total cost: two pounds two shillings. A small price to pay for / your poetry.

ROSSETTI. There is no question of opening her grave. No question.

HOWELL. Right… It's a 'no'. Then I shall not mention it again… Your neighbour's tree was full of icicles just now.

ROSSETTI. She loved my poetry.

HOWELL. We might all love it, Gabriel, if we could but read it.

ROSSETTI. We can't.

HOWELL. We could.

ROSSETTI. Disturb her grave?

HOWELL. We're not disturbing a person. She's dead. They're your poems.

ROSSETTI. It is unthinkable.

HOWELL. It's not.

ROSSETTI. Understand this, Charlie. To sanction such an act is not within my philosophy. You would have to find some other Rossetti. No poet, no artist, no human being, no man that I would recognise as party to myself would ever do such a thing.

HOWELL. I understand. The Romantic Soul. It does you credit. Though I do think you ought to spare a thought for Lizzie's wishes in this matter. She who loved poetry. What would *she* want? Would she wish to be the cause your poems are unread, unregarded, unremembered… underground? No. No.